CONTENTS

1) Introduction to William Shakespeare — 1

2) Introduction to Much Ado About Nothing — 12

3) Textual Analysis
    Act I — 18
    Act II — 33
    Act III — 60
    Act IV — 79
    Act V — 86

4) Character Analyses — 95

5) Critical Commentary — 100

6) Essay Questions and Answers — 104

7) Bibliography — 108

BRIGHT NOTES

MUCH ADO ABOUT NOTHING BY WILLIAM SHAKESPEARE

Intelligent Education

Nashville, Tennessee

BRIGHT NOTES: Much Ado About Nothing
www.BrightNotes.com

No part of this publication may be used or reproduced in any manner whatsoever without written permission, except in the case of brief quotations in critical articles and reviews. For permissions, contact Influence Publishers http://www.influencepublishers.com.

ISBN: 978-1-645425-74-8 (Paperback)
ISBN: 978-1-645425-75-5 (eBook)

Published in accordance with the U.S. Copyright Office Orphan Works and Mass Digitization report of the register of copyrights, June 2015.

Originally published by Monarch Press.
Joseph E. Grennen, 1964
2020 Edition published by Influence Publishers.

Interior design by Lapiz Digital Services. Cover Design by Thinkpen Designs.

Printed in the United States of America.

Library of Congress Cataloging-in-Publication Data forthcoming.
Names: Intelligent Education
Title: BRIGHT NOTES: Much Ado About Nothing
Subject: STU004000 STUDY AIDS / Book Notes

INTRODUCTION TO WILLIAM SHAKESPEARE

FACTS VERSUS SPECULATION

Anyone who wishes to know where documented truth ends and where speculation begins in Shakespearean scholarship and criticism first needs to know the facts of Shakespeare's life. A medley of life records suggest, by their lack of inwardness, how little is known of Shakespeare's ideology, his beliefs and opinions.

William Shakespeare was baptized on April 26, 1564, as "Gulielmus filius Johannes Shakspere"; the evidence is the parish register of Holy Trinity Church, Stratford, England.

HUSBAND AND FATHER

On November 28, 1582, the Bishop of Worcester issued a license to William Shakespeare and "Anne Hathaway of Stratford" to solemnize a marriage upon one asking of the banns providing that there were no legal impediments. Three askings of the banns were (and are) usual in the Church of England.

On May 26, 1583, the records of the parish church in Stratford note the baptism of Susanna, daughter to William Shakespeare. The inference is clear, then, that Anne Hathaway Shakespeare was with child at the time of her wedding.

On February 2, 1585, the records of the parish church in Stratford note the baptisms of "Hamnet & Judeth, sonne and daughter to William Shakspere."

SHAKESPEARE INSULTED

On September 20, 1592, Robert Greene's A Groats-worth of witte, bought with a million of Repentance was entered in the Stationers' Register. In this work Shakespeare was publicly insulted as "an upstart Crow, beautified with our ["gentlemen" playwrights usually identified as Marlowe, Nashe, and Lodge] feathers, that with Tygers hart wrapt in a Players hyde [a **parody** of a Shakespearean line in II *Henry VI*] supposes he is as well able to bombast out a **blank verse** as the best of you: and being an absolute Iohannes fac totum, is in his own conceit the only Shake-scene in a country." This statement asperses not only Shakespeare's art but intimates his base, i.e., non-gentle, birth. A "John factotum" is a servant or a man of all work.

On April 18, 1593, Shakespeare's long erotic poem *Venus and Adonis* was entered for publication. It was printed under the author's name and was dedicated to the nineteen-year-old Henry Wriothesley, Earl of Southampton.

On May 9, 1594, another long erotic poem, *The Rape of Lucrece*, was entered for publication. It also was printed under Shakespeare's name and was dedicated to the Earl of Southampton.

On December 26 and 27, 1594, payment was made to Shakespeare and others for performances at court by the Lord Chamberlain's servants.

For August 11, 1596, the parish register of Holy Trinity Church records the burial of "Hamnet filius William Shakspere."

FROM "VILLEIN" TO "GENTLEMAN"

On October 20, 1596, John Shakespeare, the poet's father, was made a "gentleman" by being granted the privilege of bearing a coat of arms. Thus, William Shakespeare on this day also became a "gentleman." Shakespeare's mother, Mary Arden Shakespeare, was "gentle" by birth. The poet was a product of a cross-class marriage. Both the father and the son were technically "villeins" or "villains" until this day.

On May 24, 1597, William Shakespeare purchased New Place, a large house in the center of Stratford.

CITED AS "BEST"

In 1598 Francis Meres's *Palladis Tamia* listed Shakespeare more frequently than any other English author. Shakespeare was cited as one of eight by whom "the English tongue is mightily enriched, and gorgeouslie invested in rare ornaments and resplendent abiliments"; as one of six who had raised monumentum aere perennius [a monument more lasting than brass]; as one of five who excelled in lyric poetry; as one of thirteen "best for Tragedie," and as one of seventeen who were "best for Comedy."

On September 20, 1598, Shakespeare is said on the authority of Ben Jonson (in his collection of plays, 1616) to have been an actor in Jonson's *Every Man in His Humour*.

On September 8, 1601, the parish register of Holy Trinity in Stratford records the burial of "Mr. Johannes Shakespeare," the poet's father.

BECOMES A "KING'S MAN"

In 1603 Shakespeare was named among others, the Lord Chamberlain's players, as licensed by James I (Queen Elizabeth having died) to become the King's Men.

In 1603 a garbled and pirated *Hamlet* (now known as Q1) was printed with Shakespeare's name on the title page.

In March 1604, King James gave Shakespeare, as one of the Grooms of the Chamber (by virtue of being one of the King's Men), four yards of red cloth for a livery, this being in connection with a royal progress through the City of London.

In 1604 (probably) there appeared a second version of *Hamlet* (now known as Q2), enlarged and corrected, with Shakespeare's name on the title page.

On June 5, 1607, the parish register at Stratford records the marriage of "M. John Hall gentleman & Susanna Shaxspere," the poet's elder daughter. John Hall was a doctor of medicine.

BECOMES A GRANDFATHER

On February 21, 1608, the parish register at Holy Trinity, Stratford, records the baptism of Elizabeth Hall, Shakespeare's first grandchild.

On September 9, 1608, the parish register at Holy Trinity, Stratford, records the burial of Mary Shakespeare, the poet's mother.

On May 20, 1609, "Shakespeares Sonnets. Never before Imprinted" was entered for publication.

On February 10, 1616, the marriage of Judith, Shakespeare's younger daughter, is recorded in the parish register of Holy Trinity, Stratford.

On March 25, 1616, Shakespeare made his will. It is extant.

On April 23, 1616, Shakespeare died. The monument in the Stratford church is authority for the date.

BURIED IN STRATFORD CHURCH

On April 25, 1616, Shakespeare was buried in Holy Trinity Church, Stratford. Evidence of this date is found in the church register. A stone laid over his grave bears the inscription:

Good Frend for Jesus Sake Forbeare, To Digg The Dust Encloased Heare! Blest Be Ye Man Yt Spares Thes Stones, And Curst Be He Yt Moves My Bones.

DEMAND FOR MORE INFORMATION

These are the life records of Shakespeare. Biographers, intent on book length or even short accounts of the life of the poet, of necessity flesh out these (and other) not very revealing notices from 1564-1616, Shakespeare's life span with ancillary matter such as the status of Elizabethan actors, details of the Elizabethan theaters, and life under Elizabeth I and James I. Information about Shakespeare's artistic life-for example, his alteration of his sources-is much more abundant than truthful insights into his personal life, including his beliefs. There is, of course, great demand for colorful stories about Shakespeare, and there is intense pressure on biographers to depict the poet as a paragon of wisdom.

ANECDOTES-TRUE OR UNTRUE?

Biographers of Shakespeare may include stories about Shakespeare that have been circulating since at least the seventeenth century; no one knows whether or not these stories are true. One declares that Shakespeare was an apprentice to a butcher, that he ran away from his master, and was received by actors in London. Another story holds that Shakespeare was, in his youth, a schoolmaster somewhere in the country. Another story has Shakespeare fleeing from his native town to escape the clutches of Sir Thomas Lucy who had often had him whipped and sometimes imprisoned for poaching deer. Yet another story represents the youthful Shakespeare as holding horses and taking care of them while their owners attended the theater. And there are other stories.

Scholarly and certainly lay expectations oblige Shakespearean biographers often to resort to speculation. This may be very well if biographers use such words as conjecture, presumably, seems, and almost certainly. I quote an example of this kind of hedged thought and language from Hazelton Spencer's *The Art and Life of William Shakespeare* (1940); "Of politics Shakespeare seems to have steered clear... but at least by implication Shakespeare reportedly endorses the strong-monarchy policy of the Tudors and Stuarts." Or one may say, as I do in my book *Blood Will Tell in Shakespeare's Plays* (1984): "Shakespeare particularly faults his numerous villeins for lacking the classical virtue of courage (they are cowards) and for deficiencies in reasoning ability (they are 'fools'), and in speech (they commit malapropisms), for lack of charity, for ambition, for unsightly faces and poor physiques, for their smell, and for their harboring lice." This remark is not necessarily biographical or reflective of Shakespeare's personal beliefs; it refers to Shakespeare's art in that it makes general assertions about the base - those who lacked coats of arms-as they appear in the poet's thirty-seven plays. The remark's truth or lack of truth may be tested by examination of Shakespeare's writings.

WHO WROTE SHAKESPEARE'S PLAYS?

The less reputable biographers of Shakespeare, including some of weighty names, state assumptions as if they were facts concerning the poet's beliefs. Perhaps the most egregious are those who cannot conceive that the Shakespearean plays were written by a person not a graduate of Oxford or Cambridge and destitute of the insights permitted by foreign travel and by life at court. Those of this persuasion insist that the seventeenth Earl of Oxford, Edward de Vere (whose descendant Charles Vere recently spoke up for the Earl's authorship of the Shakespearean plays), or Sir Francis Bacon, or someone else wrote the Shakespearean plays. It is also argued that the stigma of publication would besmirch the honor of an Elizabethan gentleman who published under his own name (unless he could pretend to correct a pirated printing of his writings).

BEN JONSON KNEW HIM WELL

Suffice it here to say that the thought of anyone writing the plays and giving them to the world in the name of Shakespeare would have astonished Ben Jonson, a friend of the poet, who literally praised Shakespeare to the skies for his comedies and tragedies in the fine poem "To the Memory of My Beloved Master the Author, Mr. William Shakespeare, and What He Hath Left Us" (printed in the *First Folio*, 1623). Much more commonplace and therefore much more obtrusive upon the minds of Shakespeare students are those many scholars who are capable of writing, for example, that Shakespeare put more of himself into *Hamlet* than any of his other characters or that the poet had no rigid system of religion or morality. Even George Lyman Kittredge, the greatest American Shakespearean, wrote, "Hamlet's advice to the players has always been understood - and rightly - to embody Shakespeare's own views on the art of acting."

In point of fact, we know nothing of Shakespeare's beliefs or opinions except such obvious inferences as that he must have thought New Place, Stratford, worth buying because he bought it. Even Homer, a very self-effacing poet, differs in this matter from Shakespeare. Twice in the *Iliad* he speaks in his own voice (distinguished from the dialogue of his characters) about certain evil deeds of Achilles. Shakespeare left no letters, no diary, and no prefaces (not counting conventionally obsequious dedications); no Elizabethan Boswell tagged Shakespeare around London and the provinces to record his conversation and thus to reveal his mind. In his plays Shakespeare employed no rainsonneur, or authorial mouthpiece, as some other dramatists have done: contrary to many scholarly assertions, it cannot be proved that Prospero, in *The Tempest* in the speech ending "I'll drown my book" (Act V), and Ulysses, in *Troilus and Cressida* in the long speech on "degree" (Act II), speak Shakespeare's own sentiments. All characters in all Shakespearean plays speak for themselves. Whether they speak also for Shakespeare cannot be proved because documents outside the plays cannot be produced.

As for the sonnets, they have long been the happy hunting ground of biographical crackpots who lack outside documents, who do not recognize that Shakespeare may have been using a persona, and who seem not to know that in Shakespeare's time good **sonnets** were supposed to read like confessions.

Some critics even go to the length of professing to hear Shakespeare speaking in the speech of a character and uttering his private beliefs. An example may be found in A. L. Rowse's *What Shakespeare Read and Thought* (1981): "Nor is it so difficult to know what Shakespeare thought or felt. A writer, Logan Pearsall Smith, had the perception to see that a personal tone of voice enters when Shakespeare is telling you what he thinks, sometimes almost a raised voice; it is more obvious again when he urges the same point over and over."

BUT THERE'S NO PROOF!

Rowse, deeply enamoured of his ability to hear Shakespeare's own thoughts in the speeches of characters speaking in character, published a volume entitled Shakespeare's *Self-Portrait, Passages from His Work* (1984). One critic might hear Shakespeare voicing his own thoughts in a speech in *Hamlet*; another might hear the author in *Macbeth*. Shakespearean writings can become a vast whispering gallery where Shakespeare himself is heard hic et ubique (here and everywhere), without an atom of documentary proof.

"BETTER SO"

Closer to truth is Matthew Arnold's poem on Shakespeare:

Others abide our question. Thou art free. We ask and ask - thou smilest and art still, Out-topping knowledge. For the loftiest hill, Who to the stars uncrowns his majesty, Planting his steadfast footsteps in the sea, Making the heaven of heavens his dwelling Spares but the cloudy border of his base To the foiled searching of mortality; And thou, who didst the stars and sunbeams know, Self-schooled, self-scanned, self-honoured, self-secure, Didst tread the earth unguessed at. - Better so. . . .

Here Arnold has Dichtung und Wahrheit - both poetry and truth - with at least two abatements: he exaggerates Shakespeare's wisdom - the poet, after all, is not God; and Arnold fails to acknowledge that Shakespeare's genius was variously recognized in his own time. Jonson, for example, recorded that the "players [actors of the poet's time] have often mentioned it as an honor to Shakespeare, that in his writing (whatsoever he penned) he never blotted a line" (Timber), and of course there is praise of Shakespeare, some of it quoted above, in Meres's *Palladis Tamia* (1598).

THE BEST APPROACH

Hippocrates' first apothegm states, "Art is long, but life is short." Even Solomon complained of too many books. One must be, certainly in our time, very selective. Shakespeare's ipsissima verba (his very words) should of course be studied, and some of them memorized. Then, if one has time, the golden insights of criticism from the eighteenth century to the present should be perused. (The problem is to find them all in one book!) And the vast repetitiousness, the jejune stating of the obvious, and the rampant subjectivity of much Shakespearean criticism should be shunned.

Then, if time serves, the primary sources of Shakespeare's era should be studied because the plays were not impervious to colorings imparted by the historical matrix. Finally, if the exigencies of life permit, biographers of Shakespeare who distinguish between fact and guesswork, such as Marchette Chute (Shakespeare of London), should be consulted. The happiest situation, pointed to by Jesus in Milton's *Paradise Regained*, is to bring judgment informed by knowledge to whatever one reads.

MUCH ADO ABOUT NOTHING

INTRODUCTION

ACT 1

As the play opens a messenger is reporting to Leonato, governor of Messina, that Don Pedro, Prince of Arragon, is on his way to Messina following his victory in a war of rebellion set afoot by his bastard brother Don John. Leonato's daughter Hero and his niece Beatrice are also present. A young Florentine named Claudio has won much honor in the war, it is learned, and Beatrice then engages the messenger in a witty interrogation and commentary on the qualities and prowess of a young Paduan lord named Benedick. It is obvious that they are acquainted, and that the raillery she levels at him conceals a genuine interest in him (whether this is love, we cannot say; in fact, the question of how love expresses itself is an important one in the play). Don Pedro and the other veterans arrive; greetings are no sooner offered than Benedick and Beatrice begin an exchange of insults. Claudio and Benedick are then left alone, and Claudio reveals to his friend the deep impression Hero's beauty has made on him. Claudio tries to elicit praise for Hero's good qualities from Benedick, who refuses to pass glib judgments on her. Don Pedro returns and, learning of Claudio's love, calls Hero a worthy lady and rebukes Benedick for being an "obstinate heretic" in love. Both Claudio and Don Pedro jibe at Benedick's "tyranny" toward the opposite sex, and he leaves. Don Pedro then agrees to speak to Leonato about a marriage between Claudio and Hero and even promises to woo the young lady for Claudio at a masked ball to take place that evening. The next scene shows Leonato being told by his brother Antonio that an informant of his has overheard Don Pedro speaking of his intention to marry Hero. Leonato welcomes the news. In another room we then find Don John brooding and plotting the means of revenge upon his brother. When Borachio enters with word that Don Pedro will be wooing her in Claudio's behalf, Don John immediately determines to avenge himself on Claudio for having earned glory by overthrowing him.

ACT 2

We see a hall in Leonato's house. Beatrice is now practicing her wit on Leonato. She might consider (as husband) a man who combined the dour melancholy of Don John and the "tattling" verbosity of Benedick. She wants no husband who has a beard, and yet a man with no beard is less than a man and therefore no husband. Moreover, all Adam's kin are her brethren, and she cannot marry her kindred. Leonato, ignoring her sarcasm, reminds Hero to react properly to Don Pedro's solicitations, and Beatrice discourses on the **theme** of "marrying in haste and repenting at leisure." The rest of the masked revelers now enter, and men and women pair off: Don Pedro with Hero, Balthazar (his servant) with Margaret (one of Hero's waiting-women), Ursula (another of Hero's servants) with Antonio (brother of Leonato), and Benedick with Beatrice. (We are not certain, especially with the last pair, whether the partners recognize each other.) Beatrice entertains her masked companion with a recital of Benedick's faults - he is a dull fool, a coward, and a melancholic. The dancers leave and Don John approaches Claudio (pretending to think he is Benedick) and tells him that Don Pedro has actually wooed Hero for himself. Benedick returns and finds Claudio lamenting his "loss." Claudio leaves and Don Pedro returns to hear Benedick make a lengthy complaint of the abuse he has received at the hands of Beatrice. The ladies then reenter with Claudio and Leonato, and Benedick quickly leaves. The Prince gently chides Beatrice for her treatment of Benedick and then announces to Claudio that he has won Hero's hand for him; Leonato affirms the match. Beatrice leaves, and the Prince, Leonato, Claudio, and Hero decide to devise stratagems to bring Benedick and Beatrice together. We next see Borachio telling Don John of a plot he has devised. He will woo Margaret at a window, pretending she is Hero, while Don John brings his brother and Claudio to observe Hero's "disloyalty" from a distance. In the following scene we see Benedick alone in the garden, reaffirming that he will never be made a fool by love. He hides as he sees Don Pedro and the others walk in and hears them speak of the great affection which Beatrice has for him, which she cannot bring herself to speak of openly, and of his own cruelty in refusing to court her. Not realizing it is a trick, Benedick does an about-face and decides to woo her.

ACT 3

We are in Leonato's garden. Hero and Margaret now play the identical trick on Beatrice. As she conceals herself behind a hedge, they speak of Benedick's grand passion and of Beatrice's self-centered vanity. They leave, and she bids farewell to "scorn and maiden pride." Inside Leonato's house Don Pedro and Claudio are having sport with Benedick's altered countenance, while he pretends that the change is due only to his having a toothache.

He leaves, and Don John enters to inform the Prince and Claudio (as a gesture of brotherly affection) of the wickedness of Hero. He appoints a time for them to spy upon the young lady. In the scene which follows we first meet the constable Dogberry, the headborough Verges, and the Watch. They are a bumbling crew, and there is a good deal of clownish activity before they finally decide how they will protect the person of the Prince. Dogberry and Verges leave - Borachio and Conrade (another of Don John's henchmen) enter, speaking of their traitorous plot, and are overheard by the Watch. They apprehend the plotters and arrest them. Inside Leonato's house preparations for the marriage are underway. Hero's gown is being fitted, and Beatrice enters looking ill (like Benedick). She pretends to have a cold, but receives some pointed comments from Margaret about being in love. In the next scene Dogberry and Verges seek out Leonato to tell him of the arrest made by the Watch, but their long-windedness prevents them from getting to the point, and Leonato leaves before he can be told about the plot.

ACT 4

Scene 1 opens inside a church where Friar Francis is about to perform the marriage ceremony between Claudio and Hero. But before the wedding can take place, Claudio tells Leonato to take back his daughter, who is no maid at all, but a wanton woman. He faces Hero with the evidence of the preceding night's tryst, and she swoons dead away, while Leonato takes Claudio's word for truth and expresses the wish that Hero might never open her eyes again. After Don Pedro and Claudio leave, Benedick, Beatrice, and the Friar advise caution. Benedick immediately suspects foul play by Don John, and the Friar suggests that word be published that Hero has died and that mock funeral obsequies be observed. When Beatrice and Benedick are left alone, they finally declare their love for one another (though Beatrice does this still with witty insouciance) and, when Benedick offers to carry out any command she may place upon him, Beatrice tells him to kill Claudio. He refuses at first, but she has her way, and he finally agrees to the deed. The scene which follows takes place in prison. It is the arraignment of Borachio and Conrade and involves more comic misunderstanding and bumbling by Dogberry and Verges. The only useful accomplishment is the Sexton's report that Don John has fled the country.

ACT 5

The first scene is set in Leonato's house. Leonato is lamenting the foul deeds that have taken place. He has come around to the belief that Hero has been slandered, and Antonio convinces him to go forth and revenge himself on the perpetrators of the deed. Don Pedro and Claudio enter and are abused by Leonato and Antonio, who promise to do bodily harm upon them. They leave, and Benedick enters in high dudgeon, calling Claudio a villain and challenging him to a duel. Both he and Don Pedro are shocked to find that he accuses them of killing an innocent lady. Dogberry, Verges, and the Watch arrive with the prisoners and by dint of much questioning reveal Don John's perfidy. Leonato, Antonio and the Sexton appear, and Borachio takes the blame for the entire affair. Claudio and Don Pedro both agree to any penance Leonato might impose, and he enjoins Claudio to marry his brother's daughter in retribution for his part in the sorry affair. The following scene shows another combat of wit between Benedick and Beatrice in Leonato's garden, and this is followed by a scene inside the church, where Don Pedro and Claudio pay their respects at the "tomb" of Hero. The final scene takes place in a room in Leonato's house. Leonato is now satisfied that Hero is guiltless and that Don Pedro and Claudio are innocent of any malice. Benedick announces his intention of marrying Beatrice, and Leonato concurs in this. Don Pedro and Claudio enter, and the ladies reappear, masked for the wedding. Hero unmasks, to the astonishment and uncontained delight of Claudio. Beatrice then unmasks and she and Benedick resume their raillery until the others produce **sonnets** that the two have written to each other in secret. Benedick finally agrees to marry Beatrice out of "pity," and she takes him "to save his life." Word is brought that Don John has been captured, and all join in a dance to celebrate the nuptials.

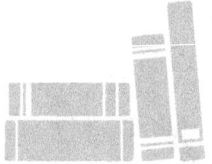

MUCH ADO ABOUT NOTHING

TEXTUAL ANALYSIS

ACT I

ACT 1: SCENE 1

The entire play takes place in Messina, in Italy. Most of the action takes place in and around the house of Leonato, governor of Messina.

> Comment: The title, as with many of Shakespeare's plays, is a significant index to the meaning of the play. From the most important event in the action (the turmoil caused by the apparent double-dealing of the lady Hero) down to the most trivial (the hugger-mugger which attends the apprehending of the cardboard villains Borachio and Conrade), the conduct of the persons of the play is indeed seen to be "much ado about nothing," a great fuss over imagined facts. It has been suggested that the title also contains a pun on "nothing" and "noting" (pronounced alike in Shakespeare's day), since

much that happens is the result of faulty noting (or observation) of people's deeds - Claudio's being taken in by the scene staged for his benefit (which occurs in Act III), for instance. To the extent that the action of the play reflects Shakespeare's own sense of the comic side of human existence, of course, the title may even be taken as a wry summation of the meaning of life, insofar as that meaning is embodied in the activities of wooing and matchmaking.

A messenger is reporting to Leonato, his daughter Hero, and his niece Beatrice that Don Pedro, Prince of Arragon, will be stopping at Messina that night on his way back from an "action" (that is, a war, presumably the war of rebellion which we later learn has been promoted by his bastard brother Don John). Leonato also learns that a young Florentine named Claudio has received much honor in this war, "doing in the figure of a lamb the feats of a lion." Claudio has an uncle in Messina and, as the messenger reports, at the news of Claudio's valorous deeds he broke out into tears "in great measure." Leonato calls this a "kind overflow of kindness" and adds that "there are no faces truer than those that are so washed."

Comment: The dialogue thus far serves the very necessary purpose of exposition, of course, but in typical fashion Shakespeare introduces unobtrusive suggestions of his major concerns in the play. The words "kind" and "kindness" still strongly imply "nature" rather than "benevolence," and by being associated here with "measure" and "truth" they foreshadow the important themes of the proper proportioning of expression to the natural feelings within and of estimating the inner truth of characters and situations by reading the exterior signs correctly.

Beatrice interrupts by asking whether "Signior Mountanto" (by whom she means Benedick, an officer in Don Pedro's army) has returned from the wars. "Mountanto" is a dueling term, and we are to understand here both that Beatrice and Benedick are familiar with each other, and that she is jibing at what appears to be a certain cavalier or boastful quality in his character. The messenger replies that he has also returned, and Beatrice makes some further insulting remarks about his "gallantry," at which Leonato chides her for "taxing Signior Benedick too much," and reminds her than Benedick is her match in witty banter. But she continues, saying that since he is such an excellent "trencher man" (a good man with knife and fork) he ought to have a good "stomach" for fighting. The messenger insists that Benedick is a man "stuffed with all honorable virtues," and Beatrice picks up the messenger's unfortunate word, retorting: "It is so indeed; he is no less than a stuffed man; but for the stuffing - well, we are all mortal."

Comment: Beatrice breaks off before she explains what she means by a "stuffed man" (for one thing, it was once a slang term for "cuckold"), but by connecting it with human mortality she underlines man's partly comical, partly pathetic position as a creature who has been filled up with an allotment of physical and moral attributes which it is his always difficult - and sometimes painful - duty to recognize and control.

Leonato mollifies the messenger by explaining that there is a kind of "merry war" which goes on between Beatrice and Benedick and that they never meet without a "skirmish of wit." Beatrice replies that it does Benedick no good, for in their last conflict he lost four of his five wits. Then (perhaps with ill-concealed irritation at Benedick's preference for male friendship) she asks "who is his companion now? He hath every month a new sworn brother."

Comment: "Male friendship" as a conventional ideal (going back to Plato and the Greeks) was a Renaissance fashion; it often came into conflict, at least in literature, with ordinary love between the sexes. Shakespeare's sonnet sequence provides a notable example. The poet's love for the "dark lady" and his affection for the young man seem to be irreconcilable (at least when those two fall in love with each other), and the poet exclaims:

"That thou hast her it is not all my grief, And yet it may be said I loved her dearly; That she hath thee is of my wailing chief, A loss in love that touches me more nearly."

This conflict is also the subject of *The Two Gentlemen of Verona*, and it is an important side issue in the Bandello story on which the present play is based. In *Much Ado About Nothing*, however, the friendship between Benedick and Claudio is a minor affair and comes in only as a device for pointing up the absurdities of that other conventional ideal known as courtly love. (This will be seen more clearly later.)

The messenger observes, "I see, lady, the gentleman is not in your books" (that is, he is not high in your estimation), and she answers, mockingly, that if he were she would burn her study. After a few more jibes their conversation is interrupted by the arrival of Don Pedro, Don John, Claudio, Benedick, Balthazar (Don Pedro's servant), and other supernumeraries. Leonato and Don Pedro exchange compliments, and Benedick gets the worst of a witty exchange with Leonato, which gives Beatrice a chance to gloat. He immediately turns to her and remarks: "What! my dear Lady Disdain, are you yet living?" Here begins the first of the skirmishes in the "merry war" between them. The banter is not easily summarized or paraphrased, but it consists of an exchange of insults and heated denials of love, in which Beatrice claims that Benedick is the very food of disdain, and he claims to have a hard heart and to be in love with no lady. She calls this a "happiness for women" and thanks God for her cold blood, for she "would rather hear her dog bark at a crow than a man swear he loves her." He hopes she never changes her mind, for some gentleman or other will thus escape a "predestinate scratched face." If it were a face like his, Beatrice retorts, it could not be made worse by scratching.

Comment: This "merry war" is the typical battle of wits, of which there are many examples in Shakespeare's plays: the exchanges between Prince Hal and Falstaff in *Henry IV, Part One*, and the sallies between Romeo and Mercutio, to name only two. It is in the tradition of the poetic "flyting," or debate, and involves outdoing an opponent in quibbles or outlandish metaphoric conceits. In the debates of Benedick and Beatrice, however, we have an essential aspect of the main theme of the play. When the conventional modes of expressing the love between man and woman have petrified into the clichés of the Petrarchan love-sonnet (poetry written in imitation of Petrarch, which uses many hackneyed and exaggerated metaphors) and the puerile conventions of the (by that time, utterly silly) tradition of courtly love, Shakespeare seems to suggest that the only recourse is a kind of antilanguage of love. Of course, experience also

teaches that genuine affection between man and woman occasionally masquerades as disdain and insult. This can be mere playfulness, or it can be a stubborn refusal to let one's affections be limited by platitudes. In a sense, this is what Beatrice and Benedick are discovering about themselves.

Don Pedro announces that they will accept Leonato's gracious invitation for a month's visit. Leonato even includes Don John in the invitation, since he is now reconciled to his brother. All but Claudio and Benedick leave, whereupon Claudio asks his friend whether he "noted" the daughter of Leonato. He replies, "I noted her not; but I looked on her" (a repetition of the external appearance, inner reality figure). Claudio persists in having Benedick's "sober judgment" of Hero, and he is told:

"Why, i'faith, methinks she's too low for a high praise, too brown for a fair praise, and too little for a great praise. Only this commendation I can afford her, that were she other than she is, she were unhandsome, and being no other but as she is, I do not like her."

And when Claudio insists, "I pray thee tell me truly how thou likest her," Benedick asks (with some sarcasm), "Would you buy her, that you inquire after her?"

Comment: Benedick is emphasizing the essential fact about human affection (and Claudio has yet to learn this), that we do not evaluate, weigh measure, and compare those we love. As Shakespeare puts it in his famous sonnet: "Love is not love which alters when it alteration finds." Claudio's concern to put a valuation on Hero has been found by some readers to be typical of his character, an aspect of it which makes plausible his later willing belief in her alleged dishonesty, and his callous shaming of her at the altar.

Claudio then calls Hero "the sweetest lady that ever I looked on," but is refuted by Benedick, who replies (in another instance of the appearance-reality **theme**), "I can see yet without spectacles, and I see no such matter." And he chides Claudio for even considering marriage at all.

At this point Don Pedro enters and inquires why they have not followed him to Leonato's house. Benedick asks him to command him to answer truthfully, and when he is thus commanded gleefully reports that Claudio is in love with Hero. Claudio admits it frankly, saying, "That I love her, I feel." And Don Pedro matches this with the remark, "That she is worthy, I know." Both comments are later seen to be ironic in view of the rapidity with which the two of them are taken in by the preposterous allegations against Hero. (Of course, it is the glibness with which some people are prone to use such words as "love" and "worthy" without any really serious analysis of their own feelings which the entire Claudio-Hero plot line illuminates, among other things.) Benedick may be too scrupulous in this respect, but we feel that there is something salutary in his statement immediately following: "That I neither feel how she should be loved nor how she should be worthy, is the opinion that fire cannot melt out of me; I will die in it at the stake." Don Pedro calls him "an obstinate heretic in the despite of beauty."

> **Comment: We see here the first of several clear indications that the "merry war" of Benedick and Beatrice is designed to point up the artificiality of the conventions of courtly love. Briefly, this was a code, first formulated during the medieval period, which regulated the behavior of lovers, though how**

far it was observed in practice is a matter of dispute. In any case, it made a religion of love, in which Eros replaced the God of orthodox religion, and the doctrines, rites, saints, heretics, hymns, and so forth, of religion found their counterparts in courtly love. Moreover, conduct was rigidly stylized; the lady was always obdurate and disdainful ("dangerous") to the importunities of the lover, who sickened and became pale and feverish by turns. He had to carry out her slightest wish, and serve her for long years, if necessary, to win her compliance; and he had to compose poems of fulsome praise of her beauty. That the convention was alive enough in Shakespeare's day to warrant satirical attack, is evidenced by such poems as Donne's "The Canonization," which makes a witty metaphor of the love-religion parallel.

Benedick expresses gratitude that woman bore him and nurtured him, but declines to have "a recheat winded in my forehead," or to "hang his bugle in an invisible baldrick," apparently a reference to the cuckold's fate which any husband may suffer - he will remain a bachelor. Don Pedro (with the wisdom born of experience) asserts: "I shall see thee, ere I die, look pale with love," but this only provokes Benedick to the vehement promise that if he ever loses more blood with love than he can get back through drinking he will allow them to "hang me up at the door of a brothel-house for the sign of blind Cupid." Don Pedro's sententious quotation, "In time the savage bull doth bear the yoke," leads to some further good-natured raillery centering about "horns" (a symbol of sexual activity); the Prince finally sends Benedick to Leonato with word that they will meet him for supper. After his departure, Claudio tells the Prince that he may be able to help him in his suit and asks:

"Hath Leonato any son, my lord?" The Prince replies, "No child but Hero; she's his only heir."

> **Comment: It is this exchange, perhaps more than anything else which Claudio says in the play, which gives rise to the judgment that his match with Hero is (as Prouty points out) of the order of a mariage de convenance, or arranged marriage. Certainly there are suggestions that in this alliance we are witnessing a marriage which is economically advantageous for Claudio, and politic for Leonato, yet a certain genuine feeling on Claudio's part seems undeniable, especially in such utterances as that in which he speaks of the war-thoughts which have vanished from his mind, in whose place, "Come thronging soft and delicate desires, All prompting me how fair young Hero is, Saying, I lik'd her ere I went to wars."**
>
> **In short, there may be something perfunctory in Claudio's expressions of love, but he does not appear to be motivated purely by reasons of expediency.**

That Don Pedro subscribes to the (courtly love) stereotype of the lover as a spouter of poetic praises of his lady, is indicated by his remark to Claudio: "Thou wilt be like a lover presently, / And tire the hearer with a book of words." He promises, however, not only to intercede with Leonato in Claudio's behalf, but actually to broach his suit to Hero herself - in fact, to woo her for him - an arrangement which only serves to underline the superficiality of the kind of "love" which Claudio imagines he has for Hero. There is to be a masked ball that evening at Leonato's house, and the Prince offers to pretend that he is Claudio in disguise and to "unclasp his heart" in Hero's bosom, and to "take her hearing prisoner with the force / And strong encounter of my amorous tale." "She shall be thine," he promises the young lord.

SUMMARY

This opening scene, the longest in the play, has a number of functions in addition to mere exposition:

1. It introduces all the main characters of the play: Don Pedro, Prince of Arragon; Don John, his bastard brother; Claudio, a young lord of Florence; Benedick, a young lord of Padua; Leonato, governor of Messina; Hero, his daughter; and Beatrice, his niece.

2. It demonstrates in great detail the "merry war" which characterizes the relationship of Benedick and Beatrice and hints at the probability of a serious love underlying their mutual raillery. The names Beatrice (blesser) and Benedick (the blessed one) certainly are not accidental, and suggest, at the very least, that the dramatist's interest was in their love and its problems rather than that of Claudio and Hero.

3. It establishes the comparative superficiality of Claudio's love for Hero, as well as the camaraderie and affection of Claudio and Benedick.

4. Several important **themes** are foreshadowed in the **metaphors** and explicit statements of the characters. Some of these are:

    a. "Clear vision" as a symbol of the awareness of the complex nature of human love. This is seen principally in Benedick's rejoinders to Claudio: "I noted her not; but I looked on her," and "I can see yet without spectacles and I see no such matter."

  b. "Wit" as the natural expression of intelligence. This is observed mainly in the "skirmish of wit" between Beatrice and Benedick, but there are similar skirmishes between Benedick and Leonato, Beatrice and the Messenger, and Don Pedro and Benedick.

  c. "Speech" as an inadequate mode of expressing what is in the heart. The Messenger, for instance, says to Leonato (about Claudio's feats): "He hath indeed better bettered expectation than you must expect of me to tell you how"; and Beatrice claims that she would "rather hear my dog bark at a crow than a man swear he loves me."

5. There are a number of important verbal motifs introduced here which will be played upon in future scenes. Two of these are:

  a. The "stuffed man" figure (here, with reference to Benedick as one "stuffed" with virtues, though there is a faint suggestion of the cant meaning "cuckold," who, as a man betrayed in love, is therefore one who has been given "horns," another motif brought into the scene).

  b. "Measure": In this scene "measure refers principally to moderation or "proper proportion," as in Don Pedro's victory, which is "twice itself when the achiever brings home full numbers," or in the tears of joy which Claudio's uncle sheds "in great measure." "Measure" is also the word for "dance," a figure of great importance in the play, and this aspect of the word's meaning will be brought out in later scenes.

6. Finally, the occasion of the opening scene - the ceremonial occasion of "reunion upon returning from the wars" - establishes the formal and ceremonial fabric of the action as a whole, a feature which is underlined by the abrupt switch from prose to verse in the speeches of Claudio and Don Pedro which close the scene.

ACT 1: SCENE 2

In a room in Leonato's house the governor and his brother Antonio are commenting on the preparations for the ball. Antonio reports the "good news" that one of his servants overheard Don Pedro announcing that he loved Hero and intended to ask for her hand in marriage. Leonato decides to be less than optimistic about this, but determines to inform Hero so that she may be prepared in any case.

SUMMARY

This extremely short scene has always been a baffling one. It does not advance the action in any significant way, except to show that preparations for the ball are underway, and nothing comes of Antonio's misunderstanding of the agreement between Claudio and the Prince. But the scene seems to have thematic importance in several ways:

1. It shows Leonato and Antonio in the posture of "overhearers," a constant motif in the play.

2. Antonio is connected with the appearance-reality **theme**. The details he has learned "have a good cover; they show well outward."

3. The **theme** of appearance and reality is also brought into connection with that of "dreaming and waking," as Antonio offers to "tell you strange news that you yet dreamt not of," and Leonato decides to "hold it as a dream till it appear itself."

4. "Wit" is also briefly mentioned. Leonato wonders, "Hath the fellow any wit that told you this?"

ACT 1: SCENE 3

In another room in Leonato's house, Don John and his man Conrade are conversing. Conrade wishes to know why his lord is so "sad without measure" and bids him listen to reason. Don John wonders that a man of Conrade's stamp, born under Saturn (planet of malevolent influence) should thus go about to "apply a moral medicine to a mortifying mischief." Conrade advises Don John to bide his time and let the good graces of his brother grow with time. But he is told (in a well-known speech, which shows the motiveless malignity of Don John): "I had rather be a canker in a hedge than a rose in his grace; and it better fits my blood to be disdained of all than to fashion a carriage to rob love from any. In this, though I cannot be said to be a flattering honest man, it must not be denied but that I am a plain-dealing villain."

He ends by saying, "let me be that I am, and seek not to alter me." Borachio enters with news of the projected marriage, which he heard about by concealing himself behind an arras while Don Pedro and Claudio were discussing it. Don John immediately perceives that this may give him the opportunity he wants of practicing mischief. Besides, he hates Claudio for having covered himself with glory in the war of rebellion. Conrade and Borachio both agree to assist him in any plot.

SUMMARY

1. Of primary importance, the scene establishes the character of Don John as a man given to wanton acts of spite. He is evil of his very nature.

2. Conrade and Borachio, Don John's henchmen, are here introduced, though we learn almost nothing of their characters beyond the fact that Conrade is not such a plain-dealing villain as his master.

3. "Overhearing" takes the form of Borachio's eavesdropping on the Prince and Claudio, and we begin to sense that accidental discovery of facts by overhearing is of the very essence of the play's complicating forces.

4. We learn that Don John's malice towards Claudio is a result of the glory Claudio gained in his overthrow. This to some degree explains the form the evil brother's revenge takes.

5. The **theme** of "measure" is here related to Don John's constitution. He is "out of measure sad," says Conrade, and he replies, "There is no measure in the occasion that breeds; therefore the sadness is without limits."

6. "Sad," as in the above quotations, is another concept that has a functional importance in the play. It can mean things as diverse as "serious," "grave," "melancholy," and "believable," among other things. The alternate meanings that various persons place upon it is one of the many ways in which character is defined in the play.

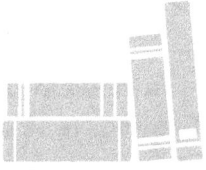

MUCH ADO ABOUT NOTHING

TEXTUAL ANALYSIS

ACT II

ACT II: SCENE 1

The first scene opens in a hall in Leonato's house. Leonato, Antonio, Beatrice, and Hero are discussing Don John. To Beatrice he seems to "look tartly," and he gives her heartburn for an hour. Hero describes him (in more conventional terms) as being "of a very melancholy disposition."

> **Comment:** Medieval and Renaissance psychology was a very schematic affair. There were thought to be four liquids or "humors" in the body (black bile, yellow bile, blood, and phlegm) giving rise to four main constitutions, melancholy, choleric, sanguine, and phlegmatic, depending on which of these predominated in the individual. It must have been obvious to any person of intelligence in Shakespeare's day that as a description of the varieties of human motive and action this was a limited theory. Indeed,

the fact that Hero is so conventional in her analysis of Don John, while Beatrice is so original, is another measure of Beatrice's relative complexity.

Beatrice suggests that a man who should combine in himself the qualities of Don John and Benedick would be an excellent man; such a man could win any woman in the world, provided he also had a good leg (for bowing?), a good foot (for dancing?), and money enough. Leonato calls her "shrewd" (that is, "like a shrew," rather than simply "clever"), and Antonio calls her "too curst." By quoting the proverb, "God sends a curst cow short horns," Beatrice wittily "proves" that by being too curst she will have no "horns" at all; that is, she will have no husband. In any case, she could not stand a husband with a beard on his face, though Leonato suggests that she may find one without a beard. She retorts: "What should I do with him? Dress him in my apparel and make him my waiting gentlewoman? He that hath a beard is more than a youth, and he that hath no beard is less than a man; and he that is more than a youth is not for me; and he that is less than a man, I am not for him. Therefore I will take even sixpence in earnest of the Bear-ward, and lead his apes into hell."

Comment: Beatrice plays wittily on the proverbial punishment for old maids - "leading apes in Hell." More significantly, her jesting about the "nature of man" is a kind of comic equivalent of this idea as treated seriously in so many tragic plays: *Hamlet*, pondering the theme, "What a piece of work is man," is a notable instance.

Leonato thinks he can create a witty trap - make her admit she is bound for hell, but she says no, the devil (wearing horns, and hence an "old cuckold") will send her (since she has refused marriage - and therefore "horns") off to heaven where she will sit with the bachelors and live "as merry as the day is long." Leonato, in good humor, expresses the wish that she may someday be fitted with a good husband, but she replies that she will never be mastered by a "piece of valiant dust," a "clod of wayward marl"; besides, Adam's sons are her brethren, and she holds it a sin to marry her kindred.

Leonato then turns to Hero and bids her make a proper answer to the Prince if he should bring up the subject of marriage. Beatrice interrupts, and reminds Hero that "the fault will be in the music" if she "be not wooed in good time." If the Prince seems too lofty for her, she may "tell him there is measure in everything and so dance out the answer."

Comment: "Measure" and "good time" are here puns on the usual meanings and the musical (or choreographic) meanings of these terms. Observing human actions and reaching conclusions about the way in which one can participate in human society are symbolically represented in the play as the process of "observing measure" and participating in the "dance" of human life. There are frequent ironies in Beatrice's witty evaluations of other persons' gullibility and thoughtless mimicry of conventional attitudes, but these are modified by the final (gentle) irony in the closing scene of the play, when even Benedick and Beatrice have to take part in the "dance."

Beatrice even couches her "marry in haste" warning in the dance figure: "Wooing, wedding, and repenting is as a Scotch jig, a measure, and a cinque-pace"; wooing is the jig, the wedding the measure, and Repentance dances the cinque-pace (by "sinking" into his grave). Leonato compliments her on her "shrewd apprehension" and, in a famous line, Beatrice retorts: "I have a good eye, uncle; I can see a church by daylight." At this point the rest of the revelers enter, all masked. (The usual Elizabethan stage **convention** provided that disguise was impenetrable, but in this scene we are certainly meant to consider the possibility that the maskers know each other. We know definitely, in any case, that Benedick recognizes Beatrice.)

Don Pedro is first shown walking aside with Hero, and it is apparent that his wooing of her (for Claudio) will now begin. Balthazar, his servant, is shown dancing with Margaret, Hero's lady-in-waiting. There is a slight flirtatious exchange, ending in Margaret's "prayer" to be matched with a good dancer, but to be rid of him when the dance is done. Ursula, another of Hero's maids, is with Antonio; she tells him she knows it is he by the waggling of his head and his dry hands, but he denies it until she admits that she knows him by his "excellent wit." Finally, Benedick and Beatrice are shown conversing. He reports that someone told him she was disdainful and got all of her "wit" out of *The Hundred Merry Tales* (a popular jest book of the day). She says it must have been Benedick who told him, and then describes him as a jester and a dull fool, a slanderer and a villain. When he is introduced to the gentleman, Benedick promises, he will pass the word on to him. Suddenly, hearing the sound of music within, he remarks: "We must follow the leaders" (that is, of the dance), and she adds, "in every good thing."

Comment: This is an unconscious irony - an anticipation of their eventual compromise with convention by joining the "dance."

The maskers dance and then leave, Don John, Borachio, and Claudio remaining on the stage. Don John accosts Claudio as if he were Benedick and asks him to try to dissuade the Prince from marriage with Hero since she is no match for him in social station. When "Benedick" (Claudio) inquires how he knows the Prince loves her, Don John lies, saying that he overheard him swearing his affection. Borachio confirms this, adding that the Prince is eager to marry her that very night. Left alone, Claudio (who believes what he has been told) makes a cynical speech about "all being fair in love," and repents his decision to let the Prince speak for him. "Let every eye negotiate for itself," he declares, "and trust no agent; for beauty is a witch against whose charms faith melteth into blood."

> **Comment: It is at this point that the serious and near-tragic action of the play gets underway. It is significant that it is promoted by a mock "overhearing," a lie, and a snap judgment. It is incredible to a modern audience (perhaps even to an Elizabethan audience, habituated to the stage convention of the "calumniator credited") that Claudio should take the word of the villainous malcontent that his lord, the Prince, is practicing deceit. In one sense, of course, Claudio's willing belief is no greater strain on our imaginations than the evil brother's wanton malice; but it illustrates in an important way the results of "judging by appearances" and this, we come to see, is one of the major concerns of the play.**

Benedick reenters and starts to congratulate Claudio on his "victory," and adds: "What fashion will you wear the garland of? About your neck, like a usurer's chain? Or under your arm, like a lieutenant's scarf? You must wear it one way, for the Prince hath got your Hero."

> **Comment: Benedick's words are an affectionate but facetious version of the "love as a military action" metaphor, of which the "merry war" is also**

an example. But beneath the surface of his words (certainly not intended by Benedick) there are uncomfortable suggestions that Claudio's "love" is a form of "gain" or "conquest" for him. Claudio's progress in the play takes the form of recognizing the necessity of taking love on its own terms.

Ironically, Claudio, because of Don John's information, chooses to interpret Benedick's news that "the Prince hath got your Hero" as meaning "won her for himself." Benedick rebukes him for thinking that the Prince would have played him false, and Claudio asks to be left alone. His companion accuses him of striking out like a blind man," and Claudio himself leaves. No sooner is Claudio gone than Benedick begins to lick his own wounds - the slashes that Beatrice delivered under cover of the mask she was wearing. He is particularly incensed at having been called a fool but refuses to think he is deserving of the term merely for his "merry" nature. It is Beatrice's "bitter disposition" that is at fault. Don Pedro reenters at this point, looking for Claudio, and Benedick informs him of the count's melancholy humor and gives the Prince (apparently to see if there is any ground for Claudio's suspicions) an altered version of their recent conversation. He says he offered Claudio a garland as a symbol of "one forsaken" in love or, as an alternative, to "bind him up a rod" as a symbol of one worthy to be whipped." This last detail he explains by claiming that Claudio is guilty of a schoolboy's fault: being overjoyed with a bird's nest he has found, he shows it to a friend, who promptly steals it. In high spirits, the Prince replies that he "will but teach them to sing, and restore them to the owner."

Don Pedro now explains that Claudio's fears are unfounded, and with merry malice quickly turns the conversation to Benedick. Beatrice, it seems, has been complaining that she was told by her dancing partner that Benedick has been spreading gossip about her. This provokes an outburst from Benedick, who has apparently been cut to the quick by being called the "Prince's jester" and "duller than a great thaw." She fired jests at him so quickly, he complains, that he "stood like a man at a mark, with a whole army shooting at him." She speaks daggers, and every word is a stab wound. He would not marry her, "though she were endowed with all that Adam had left him before he transgressed."

> **Comment: This parallels Beatrice's observations about not marrying until God makes man of some other substance than earth. Before he transgressed, Adam was the perfect man - he possessed infused knowledge, was free from concupiscence, and so forth. Thus far, neither Beatrice nor Benedick will admit that merely being a man, no matter how perfect, makes anyone an acceptable mate. Both of them must learn to compromise with their own humanity.**

"She would have made Hercules turned spit" and "have cleft his club to make the fire too." She is the "infernal Ate" (a goddess of discord) in good apparel. Hell is her natural place of habitation (Beatrice thinks of it, we remember, as being in heaven with the "bachelors"), and while she is on earth people sin on purpose just to go to hell to escape her.

Suddenly Beatrice appears, and the Prince gleefully points her out. Benedick offers to do any service Don Pedro may have for him - fetch him a toothpick from Asia, find out the length of Prester John's foot, or be an ambassador to the Pigmies - rather than have to converse with this "harpy" (the Harpies were birdlike monsters with heads of women.) The Prince desires only his "good company."

Comment: It is hard to believe that Benedick's outlandish suggestions for "service" to the Prince are not meant to lampoon the service des dames (the service of ladies) - the incredible deeds which the knights of romantic fiction were supposed to be willing to perform for their ladies under the terms of chivalric courtly love. They did these things to win their ladies' love - Benedick will gladly do them to escape from Beatrice.

Swearing that he cannot endure "my Lady Tongue," Benedick beats a hasty retreat. The Prince then chides Beatrice for "putting Benedick down" (that is, putting him in a bad humor), and she can only retort that she would not let him "put her down" (on a bed, that is), for she would not like to become the mother of fools. To the Prince's inquiries, Claudio answers that he is neither sad nor sick, and Beatrice adds, "nor merry, nor well; but civil count, civil as an orange, and something of that jealous complexion." The Prince declares openly that Claudio has no need for jealousy; he has wooed Hero in his name, obtained her father's permission, and set the day for her marriage with Claudio. Leonato gives his amen to this, and Claudio, speechless in amazement, is taunted by Beatrice: "Speak, count, 'tis your cue." He can only reply: "Silence is the perfectest herald of joy. I were but little happy if I could say how much." She then turns to Hero, insisting, "Speak cousin, or if you cannot, stop his mouth with a kiss, and let him not speak neither."

Comment: We reach certain points in the play (as here) where the witty garrulousness of Beatrice does not seem as fitting as the becoming silence of Hero. There is truth in what Claudio says, for silence is sometimes more appropriate than a spate of words - a

truer language of the feelings than speech. The problem of observing "measure" or moderation can thus be seen to belong to Beatrice as well as to others.

The Prince tells her that she has a "merry heart," and Beatrice remarks that she thanks it, "poor fool," for keeping "on the windy side of care" (that is, to the windward side, the side of advantage in a naval engagement). She then cries out, "Good Lord, for alliance! Thus goes everyone to the world but I, and I am sunburnt. I may sit in a corner and cry heigh-ho for a husband."

Comment: The interpretation of these lines has always been something of a problem. The most cogent explanation that has been offered is that "go to the world" means "to marry," while "to be sunburnt," in this context, means to "be desolate, without a family." Beatrice is certainly being facetious at this point.

In a jocular tone the Prince offers to "get" her a husband, and Beatrice (punning on the word "get," which also means "to beget a child") tells him she would rather have one of his father's "getting" and asks: "Hath your Grace ne'er a brother like you? Your father got excellent husbands, if a maid could come by them." This might be an intentional slur on the Prince's brother Don John, but Don Pedro pointedly ignores it, replying only, "Will you have me, lady?" He is too costly for daily wear, Beatrice whimsically retorts, and then begs his pardon for her tendency to speak all mirth and no matter. He excuses her on the ground that she was "born in a merry hour," but again reversing direction, she maintains: "No sure my Lord, my mother cried; but then there was a star danced, and under that I was born. Cousins, God give you joy."

Comment: It is difficult for the audience (as well as the other characters) to follow Beatrice's sudden and subtle shifts of mood. Now apparently serious, now utterly facetious, she constantly prods Leonato and Don Pedro, for instance, into matching her witty comments, and then betrays them into serious or sententious statements. Her attitude throughout her speeches is quite ambiguous. Here, for example, the offhand comment, "Sure, my mother cried," is a glancing advertence to man's being brought into the world in pain and suffering - it is almost a biblical reference, but the casual way in which it is uttered saves it from the ponderous import of a sentiment such as Gloucester's (in King Lear): "We must endure our going hence, even as our coming hither; ripeness is all." And when she adds, "but then there was a star danced, and under that I was born," the potential weightiness is dissipated. (And, incidentally, the "dance" figure is introduced in still another form. "Measure" and "dancing" are both brought into connection with "mirth."

Leonato, who apparently thinks Beatrice's forwardness may prove embarrassing to the Prince, dispatches her on some trifling errand and she leaves, asking her uncle's "mercy" and the Prince's pardon.' In a generous understatement of the case the Prince compliments Beatrice as a "pleasant spirited lady," and Leonato agrees that there is little melancholy in her. "She is never sad but when she sleeps, 'he remarks, ' and not ever sad then," for she frequently dreams unhappy things and "wakes herself with laughing."

Comment: The shifting meanings of the word "sad" impart ironic overtones to the statement of Leonato, for whom "sad" obviously means not merely "serious" but "of grave demeanor." In other words, Beatrice's friends will never understand her complex personality until they recognize that one may be "sad" (in the Elizabethan sense) and "merry" at the same time.

The Prince decides that a match between Beatrice and Benedick would be just the thing, and Leonato is tickled by the notion too. "O Lord, my lord, if they were but a week married, they would talk themselves mad." Turning to Claudio the Prince asks him when he wishes to be married, and he replies: "Time goes on crutches till love have all his rites." Leonato, however, wishes a full week "to have all things answer his mind" (that is, to observe all the amenities of ceremony and celebration).

Comment: Claudio's reference to the "rites of love" (which are not "ritual" at all, but "natural") sharpens the opposition between his impatience and Leonato's concern for the observation of proper ceremony. It is one more form of the nature convention antithesis so prominent in the play.

The Prince promises that the time will pass swiftly since, with their help, he hopes to bring Signior Benedick and the Lady Beatrice into a "mountain of affection." Leonato promises his cooperation, and even Hero agrees to perform "any modest office" to help her cousin to a good husband. The scene ends with Don Pedro loudly singing the praises of Benedick. He is noble, valorous, and honest. In spite of his "quick wit and his queasy stomach," he will be made to fall in love. And, the Prince adds, if we are successful in this "Cupid is no longer an archer; his glory shall be ours, for we are the only love-gods."

Comment: Don Pedro's closing remark implies that it will be a task of some magnitude to make Benedick and Beatrice fall in love. The scene thus ends on another version of the love-war metaphor. Cupid as archer is hence a "warrior." The (military) "glory" he gains with his bow, therefore, will belong to the matchmakers, who will prove themselves the better "archers."

SUMMARY

The most important function of this scene is to concretize the various **allusions** to "disguise," "overhearing," "music," "measure," "dance," and "wit" in the commanding symbol of a masked ball, in the course of which: the Prince can impersonate Claudio and woo Hero for him; Don John can set in motion an ineffectual plot to cause a falling out between Claudio and Don Pedro; and Benedick and Beatrice can gropingly approach one another through indirection and carefully calculated insults. In *Much Ado About Nothing* life has been arrested at a time when love-making and marriage rule the day, and the compulsive (hence "dancelike") nature of the love game described in the witty "jig, measure, cinque-pace" **metaphor** of Beatrice finds its theatrical embodiment in the ensemble scene in which all but the malcontent Don John and his agent Borachio find a place. In addition, this scene accomplishes the following things:

1. It shows that Benedick is vulnerable to Beatrice's "wit." He obviously broods about being called a "fool" by her.

2. It anticipates the later failure of Don John's machinations (the defaming of Hero) by showing how totally ineffectual he is here.

3. It brings to a conclusion the wooing of Hero. A date is set for the marriage.

4. The Prince's intention of bringing Benedick and Beatrice together is clearly shown.

5. Important subsidiary **themes** are presented through the dialogue of various characters. For example:

    a. "What makes a man?" This is seen (1) in Beatrice's opening comments on the impossible combination of qualities needed to make a man suitable to be her husband; (2) in Benedick's refusal to marry Beatrice, even if she had all the perfections of the "first man," Adam; and (3) in Beatrice's jesting reference to the Prince's father's power of "begetting excellent husbands."

    b. "Judging by Appearances." Examples:

        i. Hero's hope that the "lute should be like the case" (that is, that Don Pedro's countenance should be as attractive as the mask he wears).

        ii. Don Pedro's conclusion that Claudio's facial expression betokens an inner "sadness."

        iii. In a sense, the very idea of a masked ball - the attempt to identify partners even through their disguises. This is, of course, a symbolic parallel to the more abstract notion of attempting to judge motives by looking at facial expressions, gestures, and actions (Leonato's attempt, for instance, to make sense of Beatrice's awaking from unhappy dreams in a fit of laughter).

    c. "Sight" as Awareness of Complexity. Instances:

        i. Beatrice's claim to be able to "see a church by daylight."

        ii. Claudio's determination to "let every eye negotiate for itself, and trust no agent."

6. Again, the play's expanding meaning is seen in the repetition of important verbal figures. Some of these are:

    a. "Stomach" (and associated images). Don John is so tart he gives Beatrice "heartburn"; to her, Claudio is as "civil as an orange"; Beatrice's comment on Benedick's dainty stomach - that a fit of melancholy takes away his appetite and saves "a partridge wing that night"; Benedick calls Beatrice "my Lady Tongue - a dish I love not"; Don Pedro speaks of Benedick's "queasy stomach," which works against his falling in love with Beatrice. The choice of this **metaphor** shows, for one thing, that one cannot avoid visceral reactions - that love, fear, valiancy are something like hunger.

b. "Sadness." Don Pedro calls Claudio "sad," but he denies it, and Beatrice calls him "neither sad, nor sick, nor merry, nor well," thus pointing up the constant antithesis between the concepts "sad" and "merry"; Leonato's confusion about Beatrice's sadness is another instance.

c. "Horns," "speech," and "wit" also come in for pointed comment.

ACT II: SCENE 2

In another room in Leonato's house Don John is brooding about Claudio's forthcoming marriage; Borachio says he will "cross" it, and his lord welcomes this offer, remarking glumly that "any bar, any cross, any impediment will be medicinable to me. I am sick in displeasure to him, and whatsoever comes athwart his affection ranges evenly with mine."

Comment: This is only one of a number of "sicknesses" in the play - Benedick's feigned "toothache," and Beatrice's "cold" being two others. They anticipate the later representation of Hero's defamation as a "sickness" which must be "cured" by the ruse of hiding Hero until her memory can work through Claudio's imagination into his heart. Of this trick, the Friar says: "To strange sores strangely they strain the cure."

Borachio promises to carry out his plot "so covertly that no dishonesty shall appear" in him and reminds Don John of his familiarity with Margaret, Hero's lady-in-waiting. He can arrange it so that she will impersonate Hero and bring her into disrepute by looking out her chamber window during the night.

> **Comment: We never do find out the exact relationship between Borachio and Margaret nor, indeed, to what extent Margaret is implicated in the plot. Leonato later states his belief that she is in some measure guilty, but it seems unlikely that she had full knowledge of the affair. (It has been suggested that inconsistencies such as this may be due to Shakespeare's re-working an earlier version of the play.)**

Don John is not content, however, merely to spoil the marriage; he wants to know what "life" there is in it (presumably, what sort of fuss they can stir up to involve Don Pedro and Claudio). Borachio tells him that "the poison lies in him to temper," that is, that the exact flavor of this unholy brew they are concocting will depend upon the way in which Don John broaches the matter to his brother and Claudio. Borachio advises him to tell the Prince he has wronged his honor in letting Claudio marry a "contaminated stale" (an unchaste woman). This will enable him to "misuse the Prince, to vex Claudio, to undo Hero, and kill Leonato," mischief enough, it would seem, to satisfy even Don John's evil bent. To bring this about he must tell Claudio and the Prince that Hero is in love with him (Borachio), and then bring them to a point under Hero's window where, at a prearranged time, they will observe a woman addressed as "Hero" in what can only be taken as an amorous intrigue. This will take place the night before the wedding, and "jealousy shall be called assurance, and all the preparation overthrown." Don John promises Borachio a thousand marks if he is "cunning in the working this," and the scene ends with the malcontent going off to discover the marriage date.

SUMMARY

This short scene is a very necessary one for the action of the play:

1. It lets the audience know the details of the plot, since we never actually see the deception taking place.

2. We note that Don John is not content merely to undo a marriage, but wishes to create an "ado" about it.

3. We are further alienated from the character of the evil brother by the fact that he regards even his most trusted servant as a mere hireling, offering him a thousand marks for carrying things off with dispatch.

4. The warped personality of Don John is presented as a "sickness," and his machinations as a form of "poisoning," both of which are images which will be repeated as the play progresses.

5. Placed where it is the scene also helps to create the illusion of elapsed time between the Prince's determination to bring Benedick around to an open expression of love for Beatrice and the actual deception played upon him (in the very next scene).

6. In addition, the juxtaposition of this scene with the previous one enables us to see them as two versions of the same kind of "plotting." This device of "meaning through juxtaposition" is, of course, a favorite one with Shakespeare. Actions are made to define each other by contrast, or even unexpected similarities.

> 7. In a minor way, the scene continues the **theme** of "judging by appearances." This can be seen in Borachios promise that "no dishonesty shall appear in me" and in the reference to the "seeming truth of Hero's disloyalty."

ACT II: SCENE 3

Benedick, now in Leonatos' garden, sends a boy after a book which is lying in his chamber window and then delivers himself of a prose soliloquy in which (ironically, as it turns out, since he will himself fall in love in exactly the same way) he laughs at the folly of Claudio, who has formerly scoffed at the "shallow follies" of other young men in love, but is now the victim of his own scorn.

> **Comment: The "cynic turned lover" is an old literary chestnut. Chaucer's *Troilus*, for instance, is a famous example of one who scoffs loudly at love and ridicules the antics of his young fellow-soldiers who have been struck by Cupid's arrow, only to be suddenly smitten himself. The humorous thing here is that Benedick is scoffing at Claudio for having been a critic of lovers, but is immediately converted himself when he overhears the Prince and the others speaking of Beatrice's passion for him.**

"I have known," he says, "when there was no music with him but the drum and the fife; and now he had rather hear the tabor and the pipe" (love presented once more under the figure of music - and another aspect of the love-war analogy). Claudio, he muses, now lies awake ten nights in a row planning the design of a new doublet, and where his speech was formerly plain and to the point it is now "a fantastical banquet, just so many strange dishes." "May I be so converted," he asks himself, "and see with these eyes?"

Comment: Benedick means converted (in courtly love terms) to the "religion of love." He does not know how his present insight ("these eyes") can ever be reconciled to his being a lover.

But, declares Benedick, he will not be made a fool by love, until love transforms him into an oyster. And he adds: "One woman is fair, yet I am well. Another is wise, yet I am well; another virtuous, yet I am well; but till all graces be in one woman, one woman shall not come into my grace. Rich she shall be, that's certain, or I'll none. Virtuous, or I'll never cheapen [bargain for] her. Fair, or I'll never look on her. Mild, or come not near me. Noble, or not I for an angel [with a pun on the coins, angels and nobles]. Of good discourse, an excellent musician, and her hair shall be of what color it please God."

Comment: Benedick's final remark is a reference to the Petrarchan convention which required the beloved's hair to be blonde (Shakespeare parodies this is in his sonnet, "My mistress' eyes are nothing like the sun.../ If hairs be wires, black wires grow on her head," and so forth). The whole speech parallels that of Beatrice when she looks for similarly impossible qualities in a husband. Perhaps the most significant virtue his lady must have is to be "an excellent musician"; of course, musicianship was de rigueur among Elizabethan aristocrats, but music has taken on a symbolic meaning in the play, which contributes to our response here.

Seeing the Prince, Claudio, Balthazar, and musicians approaching, Benedick hides himself in the arbor. Don Pedro invites them all to listen to the music and, following Claudio's comments on the stillness of the evening which seems "hushed on purpose to grace harmony," he calls attention in a whisper to Benedick's concealed presence. The game can now commence. It should be noted that there is no reason for Benedick to hide. Nothing in his character, or in the action so far, makes this plausible; but the exigencies of plot and **theme** require it. It is one of the more important instances of "overhearing," and it is the necessary means for bringing Benedick and Beatrice together.

The Prince asks Balthazar for a song, but he demurs, asking his lord not to "tax so bad a voice, to slander music any more than once"; Don Pedro, however, overcomes Balthazar's reticence by suggesting that "it is the witness still of excellency, to put a strange face on his own perfection" and, since his servant continues to talk, tells him to speak in "notes." Their exchange at this point is significant:

> "**Don Pedro. Nay, pray thee, come;**
> **Or if thou wilt hold longer argument,**
> **Do it in notes.**
>
> **Balthazar. Note this before my notes;**
> **There's not a note of mine that's worth the noting.**
>
> **Don Pedro. Why these are very crotchets that he speaks;**
> **Notes, notes, forsooth, and nothing."**

Comment: Whether or not "nothing" was identical in pronunciation with "noting," a point much discussed,

there is any case some obvious punning here: on "note" as both "musical note" and "to observe," and on "crotchet" as both "quarter-note" and "eccentricity." This is one of the ways in which the themes of "music" and "observation" (or "noting" - the prime example is the chamber window scene) are brought together. In addition, the whole question of Balthazar's "crotchets" and his putting a "strange face on his own perfection," is a minor reflection of the eccentricities which keep Benedick and Beatrice from recognizing each other's good qualities. In fact, there is a complete range of eccentricities among the characters, from the "crotchets" of Balthazar to the "measureless sadness" of Don John, all represented as a lack of harmony.

Benedick observes scornfully: "Now, divine air; now is his [presumably Claudio's] soul ravished! Is it not strange that sheeps' guts should hale souls out of men's bodies? Well, a horn for my money, when all is done."

Comment: There is a good deal of irony in this statement. Despite Benedick's normal clarity and vision, we tend to feel that anyone who can think of the emotional effect of the music of the lute as sheep's guts haling souls out of men's bodies has reached a level of abstraction in his analysis which is not only cynical but inhuman. His preference for a "horn" (punning on the musical and sexual meaning again) in meant by Benedick to suggest that he is a realist in love, whereas Claudio is an impractical idealist. All of this only gives greater emphasis to the sudden about-face he will make.

Balthazar now sings his song - "Sigh no more, ladies, sigh no more,/ Men were deceivers ever" -and it is, of course, very appropriate, since the Prince and Claudio are about to discourse on Beatrice's passion and Benedick's callous disregard for her feelings. Don Pedro terms it "a good song," while Benedick (and here we are uncertain whether his contumely is provoked by the song's rendition or its import) observes that if it had been a dog that had howled like this they would have hanged him. He would rather have heard the night raven (an ill omen), no matter what evil should follow. The Prince dismisses Balthazar with a command to "get us some excellent music" for a serenade at Hero's chamber window on the following night.

The game now begins in earnest, as Leonato and Claudio express amazement that Beatrice should dote so on Benedick, whom she has always seemed to despise. Laying it on thickly, Leonato insists that she "loves him with an enraged affection; it is past the infinite of thought." The Prince suggests that perhaps she is "counterfeiting," but the governor loudly maintains that "there was never counterfeit of passion came so near the life of passion as she discovers [that is, displays] it" (the appearance-reality **theme** in still another form). She is proof against all "assaults of affection" save Benedick. Benedick, musing to himself, says, "I should think this a gull [trick] but that the white-bearded fellow speaks it. Knavery cannot, sure, hide itself in such reverence."

Comment: This is certainly a crisis in Benedick's progress through the play. He has finally come to take the appearance for the reality - Leonato's white-bearded dignity as an emblem of reliability - and is thus taken in.

Claudio (apparently noticing some look or gesture of surprise on Benedick's part) whispers, "He hath ta'en the infection; hold it up" (that is, "don't stop now!"). They go on to describe in vivid terms how Beatrice spends sleepless nights filling a sheet of paper with affectionate messages to Benedick and then tearing it into a thousand pieces in a fit of pique that "she should be so immodest to write to one that she knew would flout her. 'I measure him,' says she, 'by my own spirit, for I should flout him, if he writ to me, yea, though I love him, I should.'" Claudio then lets his imagination run riot and paints a picture of Beatrice falling, weeping, sobbing, beating her breast, tearing her hair, praying, and cursing. Leonato adds that Hero is afraid she might do violence to herself and, with superb timing, the Prince observes that Benedick ought to be told of this. Claudio replies, however, that it would do no good; he would simply make a joke of it and torment the lady further. For that, he ought to be hanged cries Don Pedro, for she is "an excellent sweet lady," and virtuous. Wise too, says Claudio, in everything but loving Benedick, and he adds that Hero believes she will surely die - she will die if he does not love her, and she will die before she will make her love known; she will die, too, if he should woo her, for she will not relinquish one iota of her usual crossness. This is well, the Prince feels, for Benedick's contemptuous spirit would only make him scorn any of her protestations of love.

They build to a very amusing **climax** now, as Claudio and Leonato offer grudging compliments to Benedick, and Don Pedro replies to each compliment by "damning with faint praise."

"Claudio. He is a very proper man.

Don Pedro. He hath indeed a good outward happiness.

Claudio. 'Fore God, and in my mind, very wise.

Don Pedro. He doth indeed show some sparks that are like wit.

Leonato. And I take him to be valiant.

Don Pedro. As Hector, I assure you; and in the managing of quarrels you may say he is wise, for either he avoids them with great discretion, or undertakes them with a Christian-like fear."

Comment: The phrase "proper man" might suggest that Claudio is praising Benedick's essential manhood, but the Prince takes the phrase in its more usual sense of "good appearance." "Wisdom" is likewise interpreted by him as shallow "wit" and "valiancy," as mere discretion. These are, of course, all themes that have come up before; and even though the Prince and his companions are joking, Benedick does not know this and is thus driven to some introspection and self-analysis.

"I am sorry for your niece," the Prince tells Leonato, "shall we tell Benedick of her love?" "Never," Claudio and Leonato both agree, it would do no good. I wish Benedick "would modestly examine himself," Don Pedro thinks aloud, "to see how much he is unworthy to have so good a lady." Then, as they walk out of earshot of Benedick, the trio congratulate one another on the huge success their imposture has met with, and they are practically chortling over the scene that will take place when (after the same deception has been practiced on Beatrice) the pair will confront each other. It will be a marvelous "dumb show."

The "conspirators" leave the garden and Benedick emerges from his hiding place, obviously having been gulled, or taken in by them. "This can be no trick," he says, "the conference was sadly borne." And his language here is shot through with suggestions of penitential remorse. In the "religion of love," he is now a "repentant sinner." "I must not seem proud; happy are they that hear their detractions and can put them to mending. They say the lady is fair; 'tis a truth, I can bear them witness. And virtuous; 'tis so, I cannot reprove it... I have railed...long against marriage, but doth not the appetite alter? A man loves the meat in his youth that he cannot endure in his age... No, the world must be peopled!"

As Beatrice enters (she of course knows nothing of his "reform") he exclaims, "By this day! she's a fair lady; I do spy some marks of love in her." Actually, she has merely been sent to summon him to dinner, which she does with characteristic insults, but Benedick reads a double meaning into her words which further convinces him of her love. The scene (and Act II) ends with their departure to dinner.

SUMMARY

The entire scene is taken up with the "gulling" of Benedick. Its great length is not justified by what it contributes to the action of the play, however. Much less space, for example, is devoted to the hoodwinking of Claudio. But it is the humor of seeing the heretic in love turned into a reformed and penitent devotee which is its main contribution. This is made even more significant by the fact that the witty Benedick, the master of words, is taken in by words - he himself mistakes the rhetoric for the inner reality. The length may be even more reasonably explained by the fact that the scene is a poetic development of the basic **themes** of the play (despite the fact that they speak in prose - for it is a very imaginative sort of prose). Some further aspects of this point:

1. Just as the masked ball is the theatrical concretization of the abstract idea of the "dance," so are the music and song of Balthazar the most important tangible embodiments of the idea of "music." Despite his disparaging comments about lute music and about Balthazar's singing we see Benedick's "reform" taking place to the accompaniment of music. It is significant, too, that Benedick wishes any wife of his to be "an excellent musician." This all underscores Shakespeare's conception of human action, particularly where it is involved with the emotions, as a talent or an art - something not to be reduced to conventions, schemes, and categories.

2. Repetition of verbal motifs - some examples:

   a. "Horns." Benedick's preference for "horns" rather than lutes.

   b. "Measure." The report that Beatrice "measures" Benedick's spirit by her own.

   c. "Nothing." Balthazar's and the Prince's playing on the words "notes" and "crotchets."

   d. "Sad." Benedick's conviction that what he has overheard must be true because "the conference was sadly borne."

   e. "Wit." The Prince's faint praise of Benedick for showing "some sparks of wit."

f. "Stomach." Benedick's "stomach" is now seen as his "altered appetite."

g. "Eyes." Benedick's uncertainty whether he can fall in love and still "see with these eyes."

3. Development of major themes:

a. Appearance and Reality. The whole deception illustrates this theme. Benedick, finally taken in by such conventional appearances as "white beards" and "sad conferences" falls for the trick. The ultimate **irony**, of course, is that this is the very means by which he will proceed to a better adjustment of his own inner and outer worlds.

b. Overhearing. This is one more example of decisions arrived at through "overheard" information, and reinforces the basic idea that the process of coming to know other persons (indeed, even one's own personality) is at best a groping and intuitive, rather than a rational, process.

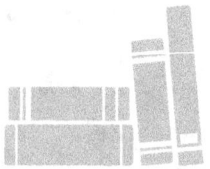

MUCH ADO ABOUT NOTHING

TEXTUAL ANALYSIS

ACT III

ACT III: SCENE 1

The action begins to quicken its pace at the beginning of Act III. In the first scene Hero, Margaret, and Ursula are seen in Leonato's orchard. Hero sends Margaret off to inform Beatrice that she and Ursula are walking about in the orchard and discussing her actions. Hero advices Margaret to

> "say that thou overheard'st us
> And bid her steal into the pleached bower,
> Where honeysuckles, ripened by the sun,
> Forbid the sun to enter, like favorites
> Made proud by princes, that advance their pride
> Against the power that bred it."

Comment: This scene is entirely in verse; in fact, the proportion of verse to prose increases as the play moves to its conclusion. The figurative language, more characteristic of verse than prose, allows for greater symbolic overtones; here, for instance, the "pleached" (tangled) bower suggests the tangled web of emotions surrounding Beatrice. The honeysuckles, so ripe that they "forbid the sun to enter," as well as that with which they are compared - the "prince's favorites," proudly disdainful of the power that bred them - both serve to symbolize the love-ripened obduracy of Beatrice in rejecting love.

Margaret goes off to lure Beatrice down, and Hero arranges with Ursula to sing the praises of Benedick and discourse on the love-sickness he suffers for Beatrice. Thus will "little Cupid's crafty arrow" be fashioned.

Beatrice enters from behind and is observed by Hero and Ursula who begin their "angling" for her by dangling their "false sweet bait." They start by reproaching Beatrice for her disdain - for having "spirits...coy and wild as haggards of the rock." They then speak of Benedick's great affection for her and of the fact that he has been persuaded never to reveal it. But, Hero remarks, "Nature never framed a woman's heart / Of prouder stuff than that of Beatrice"; she always underrates others and is incapable of love because she is so self-centered. It would be pointless to tell her of Benedick's infatuation, for she would merely make sport of it. No matter how wise, noble, young, or fair a man may be, she always "spells him backward" (that is, speaks the opposite of the truth about him). If he speaks, he is a weathervane, blown by all winds; if silent, he is a block, moved by none.

"So turns she every man the wrong side out And never gives to truth and virtue that Which simpleness and merit purchaseth."

But who would dare to tell her this? asks Hero. Not I, certainly, for she "would press me to death with wit." It would be better to let Benedick be consumed by the fire of love than to let him die with mocking, which is no better than to be tickled to death. Hero then announces, for the benefit of the concealed Beatrice, that she will go to Benedick and concoct some harmless slanders which will kill his love for Beatrice, but Ursula interrupts, refusing to believe that a lady of such a "swift and excellent wit" should be "so much without true judgment" as to refuse so fine a man as Signior Benedick.

Comment: The ambiguous nature of "wit" appears again here. When it is mere show - shallow intellectual fencing - it tends to obscure rather than clarify. True "wit" is the power of inner "judgment."

We are reminded once more of the difference between appearance and reality as Ursula speaks of Benedick's reputation "for shape, for bearing, argument and valor" and, when Hero agrees that "he hath an excellent good name," replies that "his excellence did earn it, ere he had it." The two of them decide that Beatrice by this time has been "trapped" and then go off to discuss Hero's wedding apparel.

Beatrice (deceived by appearances, just as Benedick had been) comes forth bidding farewell to "contempt and maiden pride," proclaiming her love for Benedick:

"And Benedick, love on; I will requite thee
    Taming my wild heart to thy loving hand!
If thou dost love, my kindness shall incite thee
    To bind our loves up in a holy band;
For others say thou dost deserve, and
    I Believe it better than reportingly."

Comment: This is a beautiful lyric expression of love. Beatrice recognizes her own wild instincts (note the pun on "heart" and "hart") which must be subordinated to the mastering love of Benedick. "Kindness" ("kind" originally meant "nature"') is a word which still suggests "natural" as well as "benevolent"; in her gentle yielding to Benedick, Beatrice seems to feel, she is merely succumbing to the ultimate dictates of her own feminine nature. Her abandonment of disdain is accompanied by a greater awareness of the nature of love than Benedick's rationalizations show him to have ("the world must be peopled," he asserts). And her saying that she believes in his merits "better than reportingly" suggests a depth to her love which cuts far below the level of intrigue and deception.

SUMMARY

This is a rather short scene compared with the previous one (which it parallels). It contributes to the action, to the characterization of Beatrice, and to the poetic texture of the play in a number of quite specific ways:

1. The action moves along with greater rapidity than before - and now that Beatrice has been brought to an open admission of her love, the final union of the two lovers seems inevitable.

2. The "poetic" quality of the scene - the rhythmical and figurative language, as opposed to the more colloquial cast of the scene which shows the hoodwinking of Benedick - is a fit accompaniment to the deeper, more imaginative character of Beatrice's love. There is an

apt illustration of this in the fact that Claudio and Ursula use the same **metaphor** to different effect. Claudio says merely, "Bait the hook well; this fish will bite." Ursula's statement is a finer thing:

> "The pleasant'st angling is to see the fish
> Cut with her golden oars the silver stream,
> And greedily devour the treacherous bait.
> So angle we for Beatrice, who even now
> Is couched in the woodbine coverture."

3. We see clearly (if the matter has ever been in doubt) that Beatrice's "disdain" is not the mere offishness of the typical lady of the courtly love game. Hero and Ursula speak of the "god of love," of "Cupid's crafty arrow," of Beatrice's "disdain and scorn" - all the purely conventional machinery of courtly love - but Beatrice's closing lyric shows unmistakably that her "disdain" and her love have deeper roots.

4. There is a faint (and slightly ironic) anticipation of the later slandering of Hero, in her own readiness at this point to:

> "devise some honest slanders
> To stain my cousin with: one doth not know
> How much an ill word may empoison liking."

5. The ladies' discussion of the reputation and inner excellence of Benedick carries on the appearance-reality **theme** (of which the deception of Beatrice is of course a major instance).

> 6. **Allusions** to "wit," "sickness," and "poisoning" continue the earlier development of these motifs. "Poison," for example, is the way in which Borachio figuratively describes Don John's malicious working.

ACT III: SCENE 2

In a room in Leonato's house, the Prince, Claudio, Benedick, and Leonato are conversing. Don Pedro announces his intention of staying until Claudio's marriage has taken place and then starting off for Arragon. Claudio, with more of his astonishing naiveté, offers to accompany the Prince to Arragon and has to be reminded that one who has just married a wife does not go rushing off on trips with his friends: "That would be as great a soil in the new gloss of your marriage as to show a child his new coat and forbid him to wear it."

Comment: This is, of course, merely common-sense advice, but it is curious to note that Claudio and Don Pedro both consistently speak of the marriage in terms suggesting a purely material arrangement - of a wife as a mere possession to be obtained. Hero's feelings are never consulted. Claudio has been impatient for love to "have all his rites," and now the Prince speaks as if Hero were a kind of bauble to be enjoyed by a child.

The Prince (apparently noting a dour look on Benedick's face) begins to chaff him once more. He compliments him on being a man of mirth, one who has "twice or thrice cut Cupid's bowstring," and who has "a heart as sound as a bell and his tongue...the clapper, for what his heart thinks his tongue speaks."

Benedick is apparently about to make an open confession of his "conversion," as he admits, "Gallants, I am not as I have been." But Leonato says that he looks even "sadder," and Claudio remarks that he must be in love; when the Prince continues the badinage about his being in love, Benedick draws back. "I have the toothache," he says This is followed by some punning references to cures for the toothache, and Benedick remarks rather testily, "Well, everyone can master a grief but he that has it."

Comment: The identical observation is later made by Leonato, when Antonio tries to reason him out of his sorrow. He says:

"Brother, men
Can counsel and speak comfort to that grief
Which they themselves not feel."

And he adds:

"For there was never yet philosopher
That could endure the toothache patiently."

These apparently insignificant comments do reflect a major theme of the play, namely, that knowledge (especially of the nature of love) must be earned. It is the equivalent in comedy of the tragic concept (emphasized strongly by the Greek tragedians) that "wisdom comes through suffering." Claudio's "suffering" of the knowledge that his bungling has killed the thing he loved is saved from tragedy by the fact that Hero is not really dead. These remarks of Benedick and Leonato, however, mirror an important concern of the play - the necessity for

knowledge to be "played upon the pulse" if it is truly to be possessed by a person.

The Prince conducts a mock argument with Claudio, maintaining that Benedick cannot be in love, since there is "no appearance of fancy in him" (that is, his conduct is not strange, as a lover's ought to be). But Claudio points out that he has been brushing his hat in the morning, that his beard has now been shaved off "to stuff tennis balls," and that his perfuming of his body and washing of his face prove unmistakably that he is in love. And he wonders what has become of Benedick's "jesting spirit, which is now crept into a lute-string and now governed by stops." (This means that Benedick, like a typical lover, lets his mood be expressed in **ballads** sung to the lute, but it is a humorous reminder to the audience of his earlier amazement that the "guts of a sheep" could "hale the soul out of men's bodies." We have to assume that the actions the Prince and Claudio ascribe to Benedick have actually taken place, and that he has begun to conform to the stereotype of the anguished lover.) Benedick finally loses patience with his companions and takes Leonato aside for a few words, which the Prince and Claudio assume will have to do with a marriage to Beatrice.

At this point Don John enters to spring his plot. He asks coyly if Claudio intends to be married on the following day, and the Prince replies that he knows very well he does. Claudio asks if he knows of any 'impediment" (this is a technical term in Canon Law to designate a legal obstacle to a marriage). The malcontent, pretending affection for his brother and Claudio, tells them that Hero is "disloyal"; even that word, he remarks, is "too good to point out her wickedness." He then offers to take them that night to see proof of it at her chamber window. With singular gullibility, Claudio appears to believe him and promises to shame Hero in the congregation on the next day "if I see anything tonight why I should not marry her tomorrow." The scene ends on a series of parallel comments, aptly suggesting the difference in outlook which distinguishes the three men.

"Don Pedro O day untowardly turned!

Claudio. O mischief strangely thwarting!

Don John. O plague right well prevented!"

SUMMARY

1. This is a very necessary scene from the standpoint of actions vital to the plot. We learn:

    a. Benedick's serious intentions toward Beatrice (certainly any audience would take his conference with Leonato to be exactly what the Prince and Claudio imagine it to be).

    b. Don John springs his surprise on Claudio, and Claudio falls for it heavily.

2. The extent of Benedick's "conversion" to love is pictured at great length and in an amusing way. His melancholy, his concern for his appearance, his interest in the music of the lute (typical of lovers), are all mentioned by his companions.

3. The **theme** of appearance and reality is introduced in a number of images:

a. "What his heart thinks his tongue speaks" (Don Pedro says this of Benedick).

   b. "There is no appearance of fancy in him" (Don Pedro of Benedick, again, in a speech which actually plays considerably upon the word "appears".)

   c. Don John speaks of his love for them which will "appear hereafter" even though they now think he loves them not.

4. Some important motifs reappearing in this scene:

   a. Benedick's "sadder" look.

   b. The relationship of "heart and tongue."

   c. The idea of conformity to "measure" appears here in Benedick's "spirit...now governed by stops" (as a stringed instruments is).

   d. "Disguise" now appears as the fantastic fashions in dress affected by the lover Benedick, in imitation of the costumes of Dutchmen, Frenchmen, and Germans, by turns.

5. In general, with respect to **theme**, the scene establishes these points:

   a. The typical and compulsive actions of Benedick-turned-lover are meant to suggest that he is beginning to participate in the "dance" of love.

b. That "suffering" (Benedick's love pangs disguised as a toothache anticipate the later sufferings of Claudio) is a concomitant to knowledge, and cannot be mastered by reason - Benedick is discovering that "wit" has its limitations.

c. Don Pedro's and Claudio's understanding of the true nature of love and marriage is still largely a belief in getting a quid pro quo, or "something for your money."

ACT III: SCENE 3

It is at this point that we first encounter the blundering magnificence of Dogberry, Verges, and the Watch. Dogberry is a constable, Verges is a headborough (a lesser officer); the Watch has obviously been specially chosen for the occasion of Don Pedro's visit.

> **Comment: Dogberry is the first (perhaps the greatest) in a line of dramatic characters who murder the King's English with impossible coinages, misconstructions, and faulty meanings and usages, summed up generally in the term "malapropism," after a character in a later play, Sheridan's *The Rivals* - Mrs. Malaprop. (Malapropos or mal a propos means "in an awkward manner.") Dogberry habitually confuses the meanings of words, frequently taking them in a sense exactly opposite to the right one. Verges runs him a close second.**

The Watch is not on any specific mission. We see them, as the scene opens, being assigned to their tasks. The farcical antics which the ceremonial "posting" of the Watch (which is, after all, a quasi-military group) turns into carry a faint suggestion of the motif in the main plot by which the soldierly competence of Don Pedro, Claudio, and Benedick turns into the confused "actions" and the "merry war" of the love game. There is no possibility, we see, for manly competence to exercise itself in the love-demented atmosphere of Messina.

It is absolutely impossible to summarize coherently the bumbling non sequiturs and disconnected actions of the scene. (With outrageous illiteracy, Dogberry and Verges confuse "salvation" for "damnation," "present" for "represent," and "vagrom" for "vagrant," for instance.) In one sense, of course, it is the typical scene of clownage which, in many Elizabethan plays, was only loosely connected, if at all, with the main action. Shakespeare had already mastered (with notable success in *Henry IV, Part One*) the technique of making the subplot a symbolic analogy to the main plot, as well as connecting it in narrative terms with the main action; the Dogberry scenes are a wonderful accomplishment in this vein. Dogberry opens by interrogating the members of the Watch on their merits and finally settles proudly on the most "senseless" man (because he can read and write) and makes him the constable pro tem. To his question about what is to be done if a suspect will not stand when accosted, Dogberry replies that he is to let him go, "call the rest of the Watch together, and thank God you are rid of a knave." Verges offers the helpful suggestion that in any case, if he will not stand, he is not a true subject of the Prince, and they have been commissioned to apprehend only the Prince's subjects. They are to call at the alehouses, bid the drunks go to bed, and question them when they are sober. Thieves are no "true men"; the less they have to do with them the better. They should not lay hands on them, for "they that touch pitch will be defiled" (a biblical quotation). If they do take a thief, it would be best to "let him...steal out of your company." With a final word to the men to keep watch about Leonato's door on account of the wedding to take place there the next day, and a last admonition to be "vigitant," Dogberry and Verges leave.

Borachio and Conrade now enter upon the scene, engaged in boisterous dialogue. Conveniently, Conrade does not know of Borachio's employment in Don John's nefarious scheme, and this in an occasion for him to be told of it in the presence of the Watch (who are now concealed - this provides another instance of vital information gained through "overhearing"). Borachio says that he will, "like a true drunkard, utter all to thee," and proceeds to relate that he has earned a thousand ducats from Don John. This confession is interrupted, however, by some comic quibbling on "fashions" and "apparel" (like the Prince's reference to Benedick's changes of fashion), loosely related to the idea of the affectations which love brings about in a man, and (very loosely) to the **theme** of appearance and reality. Finally, he recounts the details of the deception - how he wooed Margaret under Hero's name, how she bid him goodnight a thousand times, and how this "amiable encounter" was witnessed by the Prince, Claudio, and Don John. The "truth" of this scene was confirmed "partly by [Don John's] oaths, which first possessed them, partly by the dark night, which did deceive them, but chiefly by my villainy," Borachio confesses, at which point the Watch rises up and arrests them in the Prince's name (though it is a wonder Borachio and Conrade understand what is happening, considering the fact that they are arrested for "lechery" instead of "treachery," and that the Watch "obeys" them rather than "commands" them to go along with them). The two conspirators cooperate with marvelous resignation, although they realize they may be made laughing stocks by it.

"Borachio. We are likely to prove a goodly commodity, being taken up of these men's bills.

MUCH ADO ABOUT NOTHING

Conrade. A commodity in question, I warrant you. Come, we'll obey you."

SUMMARY

This wonderfully entertaining scene has not much action, no strictly "poetic" language, and very little explicit development of the plot; but it has important theatrical functions:

1. It creates a temporal interlude during which the main deception of the play may be imagined to have occurred.

2. We meet an entirely new set of characters, who have an important role to play in the plot, namely, to apprehend the conspirators and then delay so long in reporting it that the deception is allowed partially to succeed. These characters are:

    a. Dogberry, a constable - gifted with a kind of saintly stupidity characterized by grandiloquent irrelevancies and non sequiturs.

    b. Verges, a headborough - very much like Dogberry in abusing the language and missing the point of all issues.

    c. The Watch (two speaking parts called "First Watch" and "Second Watch") - a blundering group; apt followers of Dogberry.

3. Borachio and Conrade appear in such a lighthearted mood, and surrender so amiably to the Watch, that

BRIGHT NOTES STUDY GUIDE

> we are hard put to judge them severely, or to believe that their plot could ever succeed. Plotters totally lacking in malice, and officers utterly deficient in the most elementary principles of police procedure - all of whom flounder in a miasma of quibbles and misconceptions - create a dreamlike atmosphere which mirrors the unrealities which beset the main characters.
>
> 4. In general, the scene provides a farcical undertone to the main action. Ceremony, deception, faulty judgment, and overhearing, all appear here in comic versions of the way in which they are presented in the main plot.
>
> 5. In a more particular sense, the scene counterpoints the witty dialogue of the previous scene, which centers around Benedick's "altered countenance" and "strange disguises." This is seen chiefly in Borachio's quibbling about the "deformed thief...fashion."

ACT III: SCENE 4

This rather short scene, which deals with the dressing of the bride, shows another set of characters involved ostensibly with "fashions." Margaret praises the "graceful and excellent fashion" of Hero's gown. Hero hopes that God will give her "joy to wear it," for her "heart is exceeding heavy" (presumably, weighted with care at the responsibility she is undertaking). Margaret jests in immodest fashion, saying that it will soon be heavier by the weight of a man, and is chided for this by Hero.

Beatrice enters the room and engages in some light bawdy repartee with Margaret. She then exclaims, "By my troth, I am exceeding ill," and is asked by Margaret: "For a hawk, a horse, or a husband?" She replies, "For the letter that begins them all."

Comment: This is a pun - the word "ache" was pronounced like the letter "aitch." Beatrice's alleged sickness - her "ache" and the "cold" she pretends to have caught - parallels the "toothache" which Benedick feigns. The whole conceit is made possible only by the fact that the actual pains or "pangs" of love were taken much more seriously during the Renaissance than they are now. The physiology of people in love - the effect of the liver on the stomach, for instance - was a matter of serious speculation.

For Beatrice's sickness Margaret prescribes "Carduus Benedictus" (the actual name of a medicinal preparation), and Hero, because of the name, jibes, "There thou prick'st her with a thistle." Beatrice accuses Margaret of intending an ulterior meaning, but Margaret enters upon a long disclaimer, denying that she thinks Beatrice is, will be, or can be in love. "Yet," she remarks:

"Benedick was such another, and now is he become a man. He swore he would never marry, and yet now, in despite of his heart, he eats his meat without grudging; and how you may be converted I know not, but methinks you look with your eyes as other women do."

Comment: We have to assume that Hero and Margaret are convinced of Beatrice's conversion to love and are having some sport confuting her as

they do. Margaret seems particularly gleeful as she reminds Beatrice that falling in love is the norm rather than the exception. Benedick, as a result, is "now a man," and Beatrice can hardly escape it either, since she "looks with [her] eyes as other women do." (For the audience, this is a somewhat ironic reminder of Beatrice's earlier testimony to her own individuality: "I have a good eye uncle; I can see a church by daylight.")

To Margaret's unassailable good sense Beatrice can only stammer, "What pace is this that thy tongue keeps?" She replies, "Not a false gallop."

Comment: Here we have the "measure" figure in still another form. The rhythmical connotation of "pace" and "gallop" is another minor way of equating "love" with "dance." Margaret's speech looks back (with some irony, for the audience) to Beatrice's earlier "jig, measure, cinque-pace" metaphor for wooing and wedding.

Ursula comes in with the news that all the gallants of the town have come to fetch Hero to church, and the scene ends with Hero urging Margaret and Urusula to help her dress for the wedding.

SUMMARY

This scene is not strictly essential to the plot, but it performs several functions connected with thematic emphasis and realistic presentation:

1. We find Hero in all the excitement of anticipation of her marriage and in all the maidenly modesty which she has displayed so far. This increases the shock and the pathos of the scene soon to follow, in which she suffers the slanderous accusations of Claudio and Don Pedro.

2. This is the third set of characters (in as many scenes) who engage in a conversation about "fashions" of one sort or another, to which there is an undercurrent of bawdy jesting. The meaning which comes out of this sort of juxtaposition and counterpointing is hard to define, of course. In a general way, it illustrates the fact that people of diverse interests and drives find themselves strangely subject to the same laws of behavior; here, more pointedly, the farcical version of the motif as Borachio and Conrade play upon it is a kind of link between the Benedick and the Beatrice scenes, forcing us to consider more curiously the actual physical metamorphosis which they undergo. "Fashion" is a purely external and casual kind of change - "love" is an essential (spiritual and physical) kind of change.

3. Earlier motifs repeated here:

    a. "Music" and "dance" - Margaret's proposal that they sing and dance the "Light o'love."

    b. "Stuffed man" - Beatrice is "stuffed" (with a cold), and Margaret makes a bawdy pun on the word.

    c. "Wit" - Margaret's "wit" (of a common-sense sort) begins to appear superior to the intellectual glitter of Beatrice's.

d. "Stomach" - Margaret notes that Benedick, "in despite of his heart, eats his meat without grudging."

   e. "Eyes" - Margaret reminds Beatrice that she looks "with her eyes" as other women do.

ACT III: SCENE 5

This brief scene consists entirely of the unsuccessful efforts of Dogberry and Verges to overcome their insane preoccupation with the sounds of their own voices long enough to tell Leonato plainly what it is that the Watch has discovered. He finally loses patience with them and departs for church, telling them to examine the prisoners and bring the report to him later. There is a good deal of farcical abuse of the language,, and some measure of suspense, as the audience wonders if these two will ever get to the point. We can only utter "Amen" to Leonato's comment: "Neighbors, you are tedious."

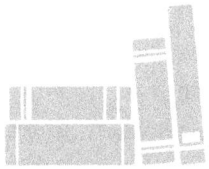

MUCH ADO ABOUT NOTHING

TEXTUAL ANALYSIS

ACT IV

ACT IV: SCENE 1

Most of the major characters are gathered in church for the wedding. After brief preliminaries, Claudio, in a very stagey manner, rejects Hero as a "rotten orange," the "sign and semblance of her honor." He asks:

> "Would you not swear,
> All you that see her, that she were a maid,
> By these exterior shows? But she is none;
> She knows the heat of a luxurious bed;
> Her blush is guiltiness, not modesty."

Leonato at first thinks that Claudio may have deprived her of her virginity and is now trying to reject her as an unchaste woman. But Claudio denies this and rages on about her "intemperate blood" and savage sensuality." Don Pedro also chimes in with appropriately disdainful remarks. Finally,

Claudio asks her to answer one question truthfully; he inquires who it was she spoke to at her window the previous night. Hero, of course, absolutely denies having done so, but Don Pedro confirms that she spoke "with a ruffian at her chamber window," who "confessed the vile encounters they have had / A thousand times in secret." Don John is also on hand to bear further witness on the point and there is clearly no chance for Hero to prove her innocence. Claudio, in one last (very precious) bit of verse wistfully condemns her "pure impiety and impious purity," and Hero falls in a faint, while Leonato calls for a dagger to end his life. Only Beatrice, Benedick, and Friar Francis keep their heads, push back the crowds, and give her air. (During the hubbub, Don Pedro, Don John, and Claudio disappear.)

Leonato now launches into an impassioned harangue, expressing the hope that Hero might die, and chiding nature for granting him one child - which proved one child too many. She has fallen into a "salt pit of ink from which she may never be made clean; there is "salt too little which may season give to her foul tainted flesh."

Comment: The exaggerated rhetoric of these speeches of Leonato and Claudio is itself the best index to the seriousness with which we should respond to them. In spite of the gravity of the accusation, it is hard to react without a smile to the towering rant of the lines.

The Friar calls for silence and offers his reading of the lady's character, based on a close scrutiny of her face and eyes. He is willing to swear she has been terribly maligned. "Trust not my age," he insists, "my reverence, calling, nor divinity, if this sweet lady lie not guiltless here, under some biting error." Hero reaffirms her innocence, offering to submit to torture if it can be proved that she even so much as exchanged words with any creature on the previous night. On the level of the sensible characters of the play the crisis occurs at this point. The Friar concludes that "there is some strange misprision [misunderstanding] in the princes," and Benedick puts his finger unerringly on the source of the trouble, declaring:

> "**Two of them have the very bent of honor,**
> **And if their wisdoms be misled in this,**
> **The practice of it lives in John the Bastard,**
> **Whose spirits toil in frame of villainies.**"

Leonato begins to recover himself and to sense the possibility that Hero has been victimized, and he swears to exact vengeance on her accusers if she proves to be innocent. Friar Francis, however, suggests a most practical plan - let it be published abroad that Hero is dead, for by this means we may "change slander to remorse," a good enough result in any case, but it may also be the means of bringing about in Claudio a renewed understanding of his love for her. Some of the best poetry of the play occurs in the Friar's speeches, particularly this description of the probable effect of the news on Claudio:

> "**When he shall hear she died upon his words,**
> **Th' idea of her life shall sweetly creep,**
> **Into his study of imagination,**
> **And every lovely organ of her life**
> **Shall come appareled in more precious habit,**
> **More moving delicate and full of life,**
> **Into the eye and prospect of his soul,**
> **Than when she lived indeed.**"

If the plan does not work, the Friar explains, Hero may be hidden away in a convent where she will not be the subject of common gossip. And Benedick offers, in spite of his close friendship with the accusers, to cooperate in this affair. Leonato agrees to this.

All but Benedick and Beatrice leave the church. This is the first time they have had a chance to talk since the deceptions arranged by their friends. Both are obviously closer to mutual understanding, though it is clouded by the Hero affair, a thing which divides Beatrice's heart. Benedick can ignore it temporarily, and he states his love for Beatrice frankly: "I do love nothing in the world so well as you - is not that strange?" But she (always more complex in her self-analysis than Benedick) can only reply: "As strange as the thing I know not. It were as possible for me to say I loved nothing so well as you. But believe me not; and yet I lie not. I confess nothing, nor I deny nothing. I am sorry for my cousin." Her further half-admissions of love only provoke Benedick into ever-stronger protestations of the depth of his affection for her, and he finally asks her to command him to do anything she may desire. "Kill Claudio," she replies, without a moment's hesitation.

Comment: This is the ultimate confrontation in the play between the conventional relationship of lady and lover under the courtly love code and the realities of human reason and emotion. Of course, Benedick cannot kill Claudio and, of course, Beatrice knows this very well. Yet there is a very delicate balance struck, in their remarks which follow, between grim seriousness and flirtatious chaffing.

Benedick refuses to kill Claudio, and Beatrice retorts, "You kill me to deny it." If she were a man, Beatrice exclaims, she would eat Claudio's heart in the marketplace. Benedick vainly tries to interrupt her as she rants on about the failure of manhood in the world. "Manhood is melted into curtsies, valor into compliment, and men are only turned into tongue, and trim ones too." At length, confused and exhausted, Benedick yields. "By this hand," he swears, "Claudio shall render me a dear account."

SUMMARY

This very important scene has many diverse functions:

1. It brings to a **climax** the Claudio-Hero-Don John action, in a dramatic confrontation before the altar. Claudio's shortsightedness and the blushing modesty of Hero (who can say nothing in her own defense) are here displayed in all their agonizing fullness.

2. Leonato, who has never appeared as a man of any really keen intelligence or genuine feeling, shows by his immediate rejection of his daughter an extraordinary failure of understanding and sympathy and is thus clearly identified as one of the group who are thoroughly taken in by appearances. This certainly transcends the "calumniator credited" cliché.

3. Friar Francis emerges as the one person in the play who has no difficulty reading character. He does this, as he says, "by noting of the lady," for "in her eyes there hath appeared a fire / To burn the errors that these princes hold / Against the maiden truth." (The eye as the "window of the soul" was a common idea, and it may be that the Friar's vision is unclouded because he is free of any emotional involvement.)

4. The means of bringing Claudio around - that is, reporting that Hero has died - is decided upon by the Friar and agreed to by Leonato and Benedick.

5. Beatrice and Benedick both maintain their relatively complex awareness of the many sidedness of human emotion and of the conflicting claims that arise from it. But the decisive victory in the "merry war" takes place here when Beatrice, with the secret weapon of her feminine nature, vanquishes Benedick by forcing him to agree to a duel with Claudio.

6. A number of images, themes, and motifs achieve their most emphatic expression in this climatic scene. Two of the more significant examples are:

    a. Appearance versus reality ("outer" versus "inner") - (1) Hero's blushing and blanching are identified by Claudio as "exterior shows" and "outward graces" and by Leonato, as "the story that is printed in her blood" (that is, her blushes). (2) The friar's reading of Hero's inner character contrasts with Leonato's consequent accusation that he is "covering with excuse / That which appears in proper nakedness." (3) The false report of Hero's "death."

    b. "Stomach," "hearts," and "tongues" (now in combination) - (1) Benedick says he loves Beatrice and will not "eat his words" with "no sauce that can be devised to it." (2) Beatrice wishes she could "eat Claudio's heart." (3) She calls Claudio "Count Comfect" (candy), and says that "men are only turned into tongue."

> In general, the basic image patterns of the play appear with new emphases and in surprising relationships, almost as an accompaniment to the emotional intensity which the scene displays.

ACT IV: SCENE 2

This short scene, which takes place in prison, is a farcical "interrogation" paralleling the serious interrogation of Hero in the previous scene. Dogberry, Verges, and a Sexton (town clerk) enter, dressed in the formal gowns of office, and put questions to Borachio and Conrade. The Sexton has his head about him and is hard put to keep Dogberry on the track. The First Watch is summoned, and testifies that Borachio admitted that Don John was a villain. To this Dogberry replies: "Write down Prince John a villain," and then, doing a double take, "why, this is flat perjury, to call a prince's brother villain." The examination proceeds this way until even the prisoners lose their patience, and Conrade calls Dogberry an ass. The constable ends the scene with an indignant outburst - "Remember that I am an ass...forget not that I am an ass...O that I had been writ down an ass!" All leave.

SUMMARY

This scene:

1. Adds little to the main action, except that it prolongs the suspense and establishes that Don John has fled the country.

2. It parallels in mock fashion the interrogation of Hero.

3. It contains mainly independently humorous farce.

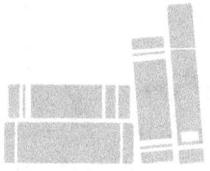

MUCH ADO ABOUT NOTHING

TEXTUAL ANALYSIS

ACT V

ACT V: SCENE 1

This scene is lengthy and relatively slow-paced; it shows various characters suffering the effects of the emotional storm of the climactic fourth act. Leonato and Antonio appear, Antonio advising his brother that he is killing himself with grief. Show me another father who has my sorrow, "measure his woe the length and breadth of mine," and I will learn patience from him - but no such man exists. All men counsel patience to those in sorrow, but they never can endure the same themselves. But, Antonio persists, do not take it all upon yourself; make those who have offended you suffer also. He replies:

> "There thou speak'st reason, nay, I will do so.
> My soul doth tell me Hero is belied;
> And that shall Claudio know; so shall the Prince,
> And all of them that thus dishonor her."

Comment: It is not enough that Dogberry be allowed finally to reveal the plot and establish Hero's innocence. The offenders - mainly Claudio and Leonato - who misjudged her so terribly, must suffer the results of their wrongdoing and come to an inner understanding of her virtue.

Don Pedro and Claudio arrive and are summarily challenged by Leonato, who accuses them of "belying" his innocent child and forcing him to set aside his reverence and gray hair to challenge Claudio to a duel for his "villainy." Claudio, who does not wish to harm Leonato, keeps his patience. Antonio, however, releases a stream of vituperation at Claudio, whom he terms (among other things) one of those "fashion-monging boys, / That lie and cog and flout, deprave and slander, / Go anticly and show outward hideousness." The Prince bears this all tolerantly, saying only that he is sorry for Hero's death and protesting that "she was charged with nothing / But what was true and very full of proof."

Leonato and Antonio storm off, and Benedick storms in, making barbed comments which the Prince and Claudio only gradually realize are uttered in anger. Not wishing to insult Don Pedro, he takes Claudio aside, calls him a villain for having killed a sweet lady, and challenges him to a duel, which Claudio agrees to with good grace. The Prince, catching a few words, imagines Benedick has invited Claudio to a feast, and Claudio plays along, joking about "a calf's head" and a "capon" which he intends to carve curiously. The Prince continues to jest with Benedick, telling him how Beatrice the other day made disparaging comments about his "wit" and his "double tongue." Benedick maintains a sour attitude, however, and finally informs Don Pedro that they must part company; Don John has fled from Messina, and they have among them killed "a sweet and innocent lady." When he leaves, his companions can only ascribe his odd behavior to his love for Beatrice, and the Prince declares (rather smugly):

> "What a pretty thing man is when he goes in his doublet and hose and leaves off his wit."

That his almost dreamlike unconcern is beginning to be dispelled, however, is indicated by his further remark:

> "But soft you, let me be; pluck up, my heart, and be sad. Did he not say my brother was fled?"

The Dogberry group now appears with their two prisoners, and the Prince demands to know why they have been arrested. Dogberry, typically, can convey no sensible information - as Don Pedro puts it, "This learned constable is too cunning to be understood." He asks Borachio the nature of his offense and is told the entire story of the plot; Borachio sums it up by saying, "The lady is dead upon mine and my master's false accusation; and, briefly, I desire nothing but the reward of a villain." The speech "runs like iron" through the Prince's blood, and Claudio feels as if he had "drunk poison" while it was being uttered. Ironically, Claudio has only this to say:

> "Sweet Hero, now thy image doth appear
> In the rare semblance that I loved it first."

Leonato, Antonio, and Sexton come on the scene and the governor rejects Borachio's confession of guilt and sarcastically "thanks" the "honorable men" Don Pedro and Claudio for his daughter's death. They both implore him to be patient and offer to perform any penance he might enjoin upon them in expiation of their sin. He commands them to proclaim Hero's innocence to the people of Messina and, if their love "can labor ought in sad invention" (that is, compose a song of mourning), to hang an **epitaph** on her tomb, and "sing it to her bones." Furthermore, Claudio must marry his niece, who is "almost the copy of my child that's dead," and Leonato's revenge will be complete. Margaret's part in the conspiracy must be determined, he declares, but Borachio insists that she had no knowledge of it, but was herself an innocent dupe. Dogberry interrupts, demanding punishment of Conrade for calling him an ass. Leonato dismisses him, thanking him for his "care and honest pains." All take their leave, agreeing to assemble the next morning for the wedding.

SUMMARY

This scene presents the aftermath of the near-tragic deception, and it moves from antagonism, near-violence, and angry accusations to reasonable offers of expiation and pardon.

1. It is significant that the insults and challenges never materialize into acts of violence - in fact, the arrangements are sufficiently vague so that the audience never really expects that they will.

2. Even early in the scene, several characters appear who are shaken out of their former inertia or self-righteous complacency:

    a. Leonato is grief-stricken and ready to do violent deeds.

    b. Antonio undergoes a sudden conversion from philosophical acceptance of grief to the hurling of outraged challenges at the Prince and Claudio.

c. Don Pedro, who has comported himself in an astonishingly genial and carefree fashion, becomes serious at the word of his brother's flight.

3. From the standpoint of action and plot there are several important developments:

   a. Leonato has learned the truth of the affair from the Sexton.

   b. The accusers are made to realize their error and folly and are assigned penances.

   c. Claudio agrees to a wedding with Leonato's "niece."

   d. Borachio is delivered into the governor's hands for punishment, and Margaret's complicity (it is promised) will be investigated.

4. From the standpoint of mood and **theme** the entire scene, because of changes of direction, rapid comings and goings, sudden revelations and changes of mind, has a disconnected quality to it - it is a kind of "chaos" of emotions out of which the final harmonies will be created.

5. The motifs of "measure," "wit," "horns," "tongues," "sadness," "poison," "noting," and numerous others continue earlier patterns of theme and image.

ACT V: SCENE 2

Benedick and Margaret are in the garden engaged in a conversation which is marked by the casual wittiness of the first three acts. He sends her to summon Beatrice and then sings one **stanza** of a love song, following it with a soliloquy lamenting his inability to write love poems. He can find no **rhymes** but "horn" for "scorn" and "fool" for "school." "No," he declares, "I was not born under a rhyming planet, nor I cannot woo in festival terms." Beatrice arrives and asks Benedick what has passed between him and Claudio. He tells her of the challenge and they proceed to explore once more in dialogue the nature of their loves (which includes some facetious quibbles about the necessity for a man to erect his own tomb [monument] and "be the trumpet of his own virtues"). The old wit is there, but it is strangely subdued.

Ursula appears with the news about Don John and asks them to come to the house. The scene closes with Benedick's comment:

"I will live in thy heart, die in thy lap, and
buried in thy eyes; and moreover, I will go
with thee to thy uncle's."

Comment: This statement epitomizes the previous conversation about loving and dying (in a sense it represents the highest kind of love-poetry Benedick is capable of). But the perfunctory nod to conventional poetic prettiness ("I will live in thy heart") is followed by the realistically bawdy phrase "die in thy lap." Like Beatrice, he refuses to limit the realities of life and love to stereotypes.

SUMMARY

This scene is mainly important for character exposition.

1. It is the occasion for Benedick and Beatrice to receive the news of Don John's villainy.

2. It shows that after a brief onset of passion, which caused a temporary derangement marked by eccentric behavior, both Benedick and Beatrice have returned to their normal patterns - with, of course, a renewed understanding of themselves.

3. Benedick's references to dying, burying, and monuments anticipate the next scene in which Claudio visits "dead" Hero's monument. It is a way of maintaining an evenness of tone.

ACT V: SCENE 3

This is a very brief scene in a churchyard. The Prince and Claudio visit the supposed tomb of Hero and carry out their obsequies. They hang a verse **epitaph** on the monument and sing a dirge, after which Claudio promises to perform this rite yearly. The chief function of the scene is to show Don Pedro and Claudio as victims of a deception (in a way, it is a symbol of their wrong reading of Hero's character). The transition from night, death, and solemnity to the physical and spiritual daylight of the final scene is also a symbolic equivalent to the main action of the play.

ACT V: SCENE 4

All the major characters are assembled at Leonato's house for the marriage in this final scene. The ladies are all sent to another room and told to appear wearing masks after the arrival of the Prince and Claudio. Benedick informs Friar Francis that he thinks he will have need of his services and tells Leonato that his niece "regards [him] with an eye of favor." He receives Leonato's permission to marry Beatrice.

Claudio and the Prince arrive; Benedick and Claudio exchange vile insults, but before anything comes of it the ladies enter with Antonio. Claudio, with great aplomb, takes the young "niece's" hand as they stand before the Friar, but he is cast into astonished disbelief, as is Don Pedro, when Hero unmasks. The Friar reflects the mood of this scene very aptly, when he remarks:

> **"All this amazement can I qualify;**
> **When after that the holy rites are ended,**
> **I'll tell you largely of fair Hero's death.**
> **Meantime let wonder seem familiar,**
> **And to the chapel let us presently."**

Beatrice next unmasks, and it appears that she and Benedick, by returning to one of their earlier combats of wit, may never bring themselves to utter the necessary words of acceptance. But Claudio and Hero produce **sonnets** they have written to one another, and they are outfaced by the evidence. Benedick agrees to take her for "pity," and Beatrice agrees to yield in order to "save his life." Benedick calls for a dance and music and turns to Don Pedro, saying:

"Prince, thou art sad; get thee a wife, get thee a wife. There is no staff more reverend than one tipped with horn."

A messenger enters to report that Don John has been arrested, but Benedick counsels them to "think not on him till tomorrow." "I'll devise thee brave punishments for him." The play ends with a dance.

SUMMARY

> Unmasking, reconciliation, marriage, dance, harmony - these are the things to which action and **theme** have been pointing all along as inevitable. Images and motifs recombine in this scene as a final embodiment of a world from which strife, deception, and misjudgment have been caused to disappear.

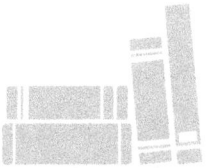

MUCH ADO ABOUT NOTHING

CHARACTER ANALYSES

Don Pedro

The Prince of Arragon is a noble, frank, genial, well-tempered man, although, as events turn out, a bit hasty to jump to conclusions. He has been successful in putting down the rebellion engineered by his malcontent brother Don John and has graciously pardoned him. He is not only lord but close friend to his followers Claudio and Benedick. The Prince obviously wishes to enjoy his stay in Messina, and his offer to woo Hero for Claudio seems to be prompted as much by the pleasure of an amusing and challenging intrigue as by affection for his friend. He clearly welcomes the opportunity for some entertaining antics in the plot to bring Benedick and Beatrice together. His failure to look into the accusations against Hero is his worst delinquency, but it is never suggested that this is the result of a serious deficiency in his character. He has simply fallen into the same euphoric spell which makes so many of the characters accept the appearance of things for the reality, and his gradual recognition of the true meaning of what has happened reveals him as one awakening from a dream.

Don John

Don John is the easiest character to describe, for we are forced to take his own word about his evil nature, and he tells us much: he is melancholy, he disdains human love, he is no flatterer but a plain-dealing villain. His bastardy would have been sufficient explanation for Shakespeare's audience of his malcontent nature and his role as a machiavel (conniving villain), though there is a partial explanation of his actions in the fact that he hates Claudio for gaining glory through his overthrow in the war. He is the necessary agent, however, for setting the main plot in motion; when his machinations have been completed he is allowed to escape - his punishment being reserved for the "tomorrow" which never arrives in a Shakespearian comedy.

Claudio

Claudio, a young lord of Florence, is a valiant soldier and a loyal friend. He is, however, one who is easily carried away by romantic notions and who tends to let his emotions be ruled by conventional attitudes. There is also something of a self-seeking acquisitive character in his love affair. He unquestionably has "love" of some sort for Hero, but that this love is a relatively superficial thing is proven by the fact that he easily believes the worst of her. He is not prone to examine his own motives and emotions. But Claudio is in no sense a despicable man; he is truly sorry for his error, is willing to submit to any penance Leonato might impose (he actually agrees to marry his "niece"), and he tolerantly puts up with the insulting challenges Benedick hurls at him, though he does, of course, accept the challenge to a duel.

Benedick

Benedick, a young lord of Padua, is like Claudio a gallant gentleman, but he is a much deeper analyst of human character. He is baffled by the emotions which seize him when he confronts Beatrice, and he rejects all **clichés** as a means of defining them. He would rather express himself in witty paradoxes. When his friends' plot succeeds in convincing him of Beatrice's affection, and he falls in love, he falls hard and begins to affect the moods and fancies of the young lovers whose conduct he had felt himself to be above. But he recovers his presence of mind and does express his love for Beatrice (though always with the qualifications that his intelligence demands) and eventually marries her.

Leonato

Leonato, the governor of Messina, is in some ways a typical stage "old man." He is interested in an advantageous marriage for his daughter, and yet he seems to lack real feeling for her and understanding of her. He believes the accusation against her, although, with some prodding from the Friar, he does finally suspect that she might be the victim of a deception. When this happens he becomes a raging avenger, though his vengeance comes to naught and ultimately takes the form of the satisfaction of springing a surprise on Claudio (the "new bride" he arranges for Claudio turns out to be Hero after all).

Antonio

Leonato's brother is a relatively unimportant character, who goes along with Leonato's intentions. He does try to assuage

Leonato's grief by counseling him to be philosophical about it, but moments later he is in a fit of intemperate rage at the accusers, Don Pedro and Claudio.

Borachio and Conrade

Don John's henchmen can be distinguished slightly. Conrade is a more amiable man, who advises his master to use reason to overcome his sadness. (In this respect he anticipates the later advice which Antonio gives to Leonato.) Borachio is a more willing instrument of evil. Both, however, promise full assistance in the plot. When they are arrested by Dogberry's Watch they offer no resistance at all and actually confess rather freely. They are merely a necessary means of getting the plot business accomplished, and their motives have their being in the same atmosphere of unreality as those of the major characters.

Friar Francis

The Friar is a sane, patient, likeable man. By advising the ruse of Hero's "death" he is the means of bringing about the final resolution in just the form it takes. His understanding of Hero's character shows him to be a pillar of reason and common sense amid a fog of deception and self-deception.

Dogberry, Verges, and the Watch

Collectively, this constabulary group is a verbose, stupid, and ineffectual bunch. Their farcical bumbling around in the night and their absurd "interrogation" of the plotters reflect the comic misunderstandings of the main characters - but they do apprehend the villains.

Hero

Hero is a model of speechless modesty. She has very little to say or do in the play. She does, of course, carry out the deception on Beatrice, but her biggest moment is her rejection at the altar when she swoons, blushes, and blanches by turns. There is every reason to believe that she does love Claudio, but her inability to be articulate about it is clearly the limitation she suffers under.

Beatrice

Beatrice, Leonato's niece, is clearly the most significant character in the play. She is a kind of dramatic essence of woman's feminine nature, especially as that nature appears during the seasons of wooing and wedding. Her "wit" masks a penetrating intelligence. It is true that she is taken in by the plot her friends carry out, and that she falls in love with Benedick, but she always retains some degree of balance and sanity. Beatrice has an enormous degree of sensibility; she is obviously the victor in the "merry war" or combat of wit with Benedick.

Minor Characters

In addition to the Sexton, the Messenger, and the Boy who appears briefly, there are Ursula (a gentlewoman attending on Hero), Balthasar (a follower of Don Pedro), and Margaret (another lady who waits on Hero, and who is the unwitting accomplice of Borachio in the slanderous plot against her).

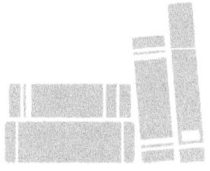

MUCH ADO ABOUT NOTHING

CRITICAL COMMENTARY

Much Ado About Nothing has always been among the most popular of Shakespearian comedies, though it is notoriously difficult to act primarily because of the flashing wit and obscure quibbles which pass between Benedick and Beatrice. Literary criticism has tended from the earliest times to center on two things: (1) the question of the propriety of the near-tragic events in a comic play; (2) the question of the plot center - is the Hero-Claudio plot or the Benedick-Beatrice plot the dramatist's primary interest?

The earliest commentators commend Shakespeare for the variety and naturalness he gives to his characters, and they consistently praise and gentility and genuine love of Beatrice and Benedick and the touching pathos of the scene in which Hero swoons at the altar, although voices are raised from time to time objecting to the mingling of comic and tragic effects. Swinburne, however, thought it Shakespeare's finest play "for absolute power of composition, for faultless balance, and blameless rectitude of design," though he felt that Claudio got a better fate than he deserved.

E. K. Chambers (1925) found Swinburne's praise ill-placed and found no "harmony of atmosphere" in the mixing of tragic and comic scenes. He concluded that "the triumph of comedy in *Much Ado About Nothing* means... that the things which happen between Claudio and Hero have to stand the test of a much closer comparison with the standard of reality than they were designed to bear." Georg Brandes (1927) overcame his distaste for the artificialities of Shakespeare's main plot through his appreciation of the intrigue of Beatrice and Benedick. He calls Beatrice "a great lady of the Renaissance" and praises the poet's "masterly psychological observation" and "delicate ingenuity." G. Wilson Knight (1932), one of the earliest students of image-patterns in Shakespeare, thought the heavy emphasis on birds, music, and dance (despite the direction of the plot) portended a happy outcome: "Discord, death, and tempest are set against unity, love, and music."

The historical approach to Shakespeare's meaning can be seen in G. B. Harrison's (1933) comparison of incidents in the plot with contemporary events - the homecoming with the return of English veterans from Cadiz in 1596, and the Dogberry scenes with the insufficiencies of the London constabulary of the day. H. B. Charlton, in his very influential book *Shakespearian Comedy* (1938) notes with disapproval that the structure of the play makes the "sub-plot much more significant than the main plot." Mark Van Doren (1939), however, finds that the dramatist did, in fact, consider the two stories together and "did with ingenuity maintain them in a relation of mutual support." The serious situation, he feels, is what gives so much importance to Benedick and Beatrice. Dogberry and Verges, Van Doren notes, "though their dunderheadedness remains indefinable," are a way of guiding the audience's feelings about the main characters. George Gordon, on the contrary, though he discovers the Dogberry scenes to be "a profound and awful revelation of the official mind," is forced to conclude that the horseplay is a mere concession to popular taste.

Donald Stauffer (1949) regards *Much Ado About Nothing* as Shakespeare's "severest criticism to date of the weaknesses lying in romantic love" and finds a serious attitude underlying the wit. "The wedding promises more stability and happiness than in any of Shakespeare's previous imaginings." Serious critical analysis of the play has been greatly aided by the study of C. T. Prouty, *The Sources of Much Ado About Nothing* (1950). Prouty finds the essential meaning of the play a result of Shakespeare's "reaction" to his sources. Instead of romantic lovers we have two couples completely opposed to the romantic tradition. It is "high comedy, wherein the frailty of human pretensions is humorously revealed."

M. C. Bradbrook, in *Shakespeare and Elizabethan Poetry* (1951), comments very aptly on Shakespeare's ability to transform literary **conventions** in such a way as to reveal the essential human feeling underneath. "To make the relationship between the two lovers display itself through the wit-combat of courtly love, by the simple process of extending the role of 'unwilling' lover to the lady as well as the gentleman was a stroke of genius." The variety of mood and tone, this critic feels, "is marked by a strict control."

The play, of course, poses many questions of scholarly interpretation, and analysis of this sort is going on apace. Some recent examples may be found in articles by: K. Neill (in *Shakespeare Quarterly*, 1952), which discovers more redeeming features in Claudio's character than recent critics have been willing to see; D. C. Hockey (in *Shakespeare Quarterly*, 1957), who interprets the unity of the play as dependent on the **theme** of "noting" or observing; Allan Gilbert (*Philological Quarterly*, 1961), who demonstrates, by analyzing Shakespeare's adaptation of a plot element borrowed from Ariosto, the dramatist's sense for "popular effect" as well as for plot unity.

Two of the most stimulating critical discussions in recent years are those by Francis Fergusson (*The Human Image in Dramatic Literature*, 1957) and John Dover Wilson (*Shakespeare's Happy Comedies*, 1962). Fergusson places heavy emphasis on the thematic importance of the "festive occasion" and throws light on the manner in which meaning is provided by analogy rather than by discursive statement. This is substantially the point of view of Fergusson's more widely known book, *The Idea of a Theatre*. Wilson addresses himself (specifically by attacking the earlier position of E. K. Chambers) to the vexed question of the plot center. He finds Benedick and Beatrice the outstanding figures of the play and sees Dogberry as having just as great an importance. The basic pattern of *Much Ado About Nothing*, Wilson states, is based on eavesdropping and disguises, "generally in fun and with a comic upshot."

This is, of course, only the smallest sampling of the wide variety of material available on Shakespeare's comic plays. Students would do well to read further in such basic studies as Charlton's *Shakespearian Comedy* (1938), Palmers' *Comic Characters of Shakespeare* (1946), and Barber's *Shakespeare's Festive Comedy* (1959).

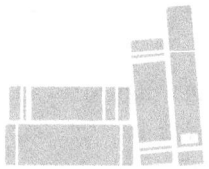

MUCH ADO ABOUT NOTHING

ESSAY QUESTIONS AND ANSWERS

Question: What is the significance of Antonio's tirade against the Prince and Claudio in Act V, Scene 1?

Answer: Leonato has given in to an overwhelming grief and Antonio has been counseling a wiser course of action, calling his brother's emotion childish and fruitless. We are reminded first of all of the opening scene in which Leonato spoke of a countrymen's tears of joy as a "kind overflow of kindness," emphasizing the fact that emotion is one thing - reason another. It is easy enough for Antonio to advise his brother to control his grief, but as soon as his own emotions become involved - when he begins to feel the loss of Hero (as indicated by his words, "God knows I loved my niece; and she is dead, slandered to death by villains") - he himself gives way to uncontrollable outbursts of grief and anger. Conrade's advice to Don John to control his melancholy by reason is another instance of the same idea, and there are comic versions of it in the advice Benedick receives from the Prince and Claudio about his "toothache," and which Beatrice receives from Margaret about her "cold." These all reflect the major idea that human emotions of every kind (love, as well as grief or melancholy) cannot be totally mastered by reason and form an undertone to the antithesis between the "reasonable" approach to love which is Claudio's and the stormy emotional bouts of Benedick.

Question: Comment on the thematic importance of "war" **imagery** in the play.

Answer: The basic situation - the background, which is frequently more implicit than explicit - often provides a meaningful element in story and drama. The Prince and his followers are returning from war. They have been victorious, and Claudio, especially, has won great glory in the overthrow of Don John. This is typically and conventionally the role of the male of the species - to do battle and win victories. But for partly obscure psychological reasons man's attempts to win a fair lady have also been consistently depicted in literature as a conflict or war of some kind. (*The Romance of the Rose*, the classic medieval poem on the psychology of love, represents it as a struggle to gain entrance to a fortified garden.) Man makes a mistake when he thinks that the psychology of war and of love are the same, however. The merry war," with its "actions," and its "skirmishes of wit" between Benedick and Beatrice, is a way of illustrating with delicate **irony** that woman has armor and artillery that can outdo man's, and it emphasizes the limitations of a lover like Claudio, who imagines that by parleys, concessions, and treaties one can enter into a lasting and healthy relationship with his natural "enemy" in the battle of love (woman - whose instincts are quite difficult for man to grasp).

Question: What is the dramatic function of the masked ball in Act II, Scene 1?

Answer: For one thing, the ball is a way of focusing theatrical attention on the ideas of disguise, deception, music, and dance, which figure so prominently in the plot of the play. The rhythms and graceful dance steps are symbolic suggestions of the ordered patterns of behavior to which the members of society (in the world of comedy) must eventually conform. Practically speaking, the ball is useful merely as fulfilling the promise of festivities made at the beginning of the play. More particularly, it provides an excellent occasion for the witty engagements (especially of Benedick and Beatrice) characteristic of the play's action, and it makes possible Don John's planting of the seeds of suspicion in the mind of Claudio. In the most general sense, the phantasmagoric scene of shifting forms and colors underlines the dreamlike unreality of the world of Messina in which these improbable deceptions take place.

Question: Define the major **theme** of the play.

Answer: The meaning of *Much Ado About Nothing* seems to fall somewhere between two extremes: (1) a witty insouciance born of the recognition that persons are swept into violent passions and come to neartragic consequences because of a combination of occasions, accidents, and casual emotions which, in the clear light of day, are seen to be trivial indeed; (2) a more serious conception that the proper conduct of life and love must be characterized by the ideal of "measure," when that term is understood in its fullest sense - order, rhythm, conformity to pattern ("measure" as a dance), restraint, common sense, and satisfaction with reasonable success ("measure" as moderation). In the final analysis, of course, no play of Shakespeare's will submit itself to these kinds of definitions; there is a sense in which the play displays the very ambiguity of love itself, which has its starkly serious moments and its comically light ones.

Question: Mention some particular instances in the play of "much ado about nothing."

Answer: There are many examples of this motif:

a. Claudio's groundless suspicion that Don Pedro is deceiving him.

b. The challenges Leonato and Antonio hurl at the Prince and Claudio, which are of course never acted upon.

c. The estrangement of Benedick and Claudio, marked by violent insults - in the end they are reconciled, and even at the very height of their disaffection Claudio (apparently) has been carrying about in his pocket a sonnet that Benedick has penned, so that he can spring it on him in public and force him to admit his love for Beatrice.

These and instances of a similar kind help to establish the basic atmosphere of the play and to mitigate the possibility that the audience might seriously believe that any painful misadventure will be allowed to go uncorrected.

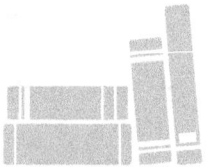

BIBLIOGRAPHY

EDITIONS

Any advanced scholarly study of *Much Ado About Nothing* must make considerable use of the volume *Much Ado About Nothing* (Volume XII) in the New Variorum Edition of Shakespeare edited by H. H. Furness, 1899. There are several useful and inexpensive student's editions, notably one in the Croft's Classics series by C. T. Prouty, having a brief authoritative introduction.

INTRODUCTORY WORKS ON LIFE, BACKGROUND, AND STUDIES

Chute, Marchette, *Shakespeare of London* (1949).

Granville-Barker, Harley, and Harrison, G. B., *A Companion to Shakespeare Studies* (1934).

Tillyard, E. M. W., *The Elizabethan World Picture* (1942).

Wilson, John Dover, *Life in Shakespeare's England* (1911).

FURTHER READINGS ON SHAKESPEARE AND ON MUCH ADO ABOUT NOTHING

Baldwin, T., *Shakespeare's Five-Act Structure* (1948).

Barber, C. L., *Shakespeare's Festive Comedy* (1959).

Brandes, Georg, *Shakespeare* (1927): more a curiosity than a reliable guide, but makes some interesting points.

Bullough, Geoffrey (ed.), *Narrative and Dramatic Sources of Shakespeare* (1962).

Campbell, Oscar J., *Shakespeare's **Satire*** (1943).

Chambers, E. K., *Shakespeare: A Survey* (1925).

Charlton, H. B., *Shakespearian Comedy* (1938).

Coleridge, Samuel T., *Coleridge's Shakespearian Criticism* (1930).

Gordon, George, *Shakespearian Comedy and Other Studies* (1944).

Granville-Barker, Harley, *Prefaces to Shakespeare* (1946).

Hazlitt, William, *Characters of Shakespeare's Plays* (1870).

Holzknecht, Karl J., *The Backgrounds of Shakespeare's Plays* (1950).

Joseph, Sister Miriam, *Shakespeare's Use of the Arts of Language* (1946).

Palmer, John, *Comic Characters of Shakespeare* (1946): has a study of Benedick and Beatrice.

Parrott, Thomas M., *Shakespearean Comedy* (1949).

Prouty, C. T., *The Sources of Much Ado About Nothing* (1950).

Spurgeon, Caroline, *Shakespeare's **Imagery*** (1935).

Van Doren, Mark, *Shakespeare* (1939).

Wilson, J. Dover, *Shakespeare's Happy Comedies* (1962).

READINGS IN CRITICAL METHODS AS APPLIED TO SHAKESPEARE

These are books and articles which, while they are not directly concerned with *Much Ado About Nothing*, illustrate a wide range of possible ways of approaching Shakespeare's plays. The student would do well to consider the ways in which he might apply the methods used by these authors to the analysis of this play.

Auerbach, Erich, *Mimesis* (1953), Chapter 13, "The Weary Prince."

Brooks, Cleanth, *The Well-Wrought Urn* (1947), Chapter 2, "The Naked Babe and the Cloak of Manliness."

Downer, Alan S., "The Life of Our Design: The Function of **Imagery** in the Poetic Drama," in *Shakespeare: Modern Essays in Criticism*, ed. Leonard Dean (1957).

Empson, William, *The Structure of Complex Words* (1951); chapters on "fool" in Lear and 'honest" in Othello.

Fergusson, Francis, *The Human Image in Dramatic Literature* (1957), Part II, "Shakespeare."

_____ *The Idea of a Theatre* (1949), Chapter 4, "*Hamlet*, Prince of Denmark"; the Analogy of Action.

Granville-Barker, Harley, *On Dramatic Method* (1956), Chapter 3, "Shakespeare's Progress."

Kitto, H. D. F., *Form and Meaning in Drama* (1956), Chapter 9, "*Hamlet.*"

SUGGESTED RESEARCH PAPERS

1. Shakespeares' use of sources in *Much Ado About Nothing*.
See: a. Bullough, *Sources* b. *The Variorum Edition*

Read the original sources for the play; study the alterations Shakespeare made in them - the shaping art he used in adapting them. What, for example, has he done with the characters of Don John (simply a "minister of wickedness" in Bandello)? How has he treated the figure of Girondo is recasting him as Benedick? Write a paper analyzing in detail his handling of one (or more) of the sources.

2. **Imagery** as a contribution to the meaning of the play.
See: a. Spurgeon, *Shakespeare's Imagery*
 b. Downer, "The Life of Our Design"
 c. Brooks, "The Naked Babe"

Select what appears to be a dominant image in the play (the image of sickness, birds, or eating, for example) and try to define as accurately as possible the contribution this makes to the total meaning. Or analyze the image-complex which results from the repetition of related images, for example, "eyes," "sight," and "covers."

3. The function of the double plot.

See: a. Empson, *Some Versions of Pastoral*
   b. Brooks and Heilman, *Understanding Drama*
   c. Fergusson, *Idea of a Theatre*

Try to analyze the relationship between the main plot and the Benedick-Beatrice **episodes** or between the Dogberry scenes and the main plot. Is it one of analogy? contrast? At what points in the action do the plots merge? Where do the sharpest juxtapositions occur? With what effect?

4. The dramatic importance of farcical scenes (this is of course related to the double plot idea).

See: a. Empson, *Versions of Pastoral*
   b. Kitto, *Form and Meaning*
   c. Baldwin, *Five-Act Structure*

Consider in detail such scenes as the "interrogation" of the prisoners or the luckless attempt of Dogberry and Verges to report their findings to Leonato. Do these have a function beyond humor for its own sake? Is there any "nonsense" which is truly without meaning or are there parallels to be discovered with events or characters in the main plot? How do they help to create the illusion of a realistic passage of time?

5. The **themes** of the play as related to a background of literary **conventions** derived from romantic (courtly) love.

See: a. C. S. Lewis, *The Allegory of Love* (1936)
   b. Denis de Rougemont, *Love in the Western World* (1940)

How do the two couples each reflect an interpretation of the stilted attitudes of courtly love? What particular gestures, actions, or statements made by any of the characters are intended to suggest the **clichés** of courtly love? Compare *Much Ado About Nothing* with any other romantic comedy of Shakespeare's with respect to his treatment of love.

6. The dramatic importance of special devices such as songs, the masked ball, the "ensemble" scenes (the homecoming, the weddings), the stylized symbolism of the "visit to the tomb."

See: a. Downer, "The Life of Our Design"
   b. Brooks, "The Naked Babe"
   c. Brooks and Heilman, *Understanding Drama*
   d. Especially, Fergusson, *Idea of a Theatre*

How do songs (for instance Balthasar's or Benedick's song) contribute to the plot? to symbolic meaning? What about the "martial" vocabulary of Beatrice? The almost formal correctness of the combats of wit? In general what do particular formal structures in the play have to do with the meaning?

7. An analysis of important puns and multi-leveled images.

See: a. Empson, *Complex Words*
   b. Empson, *Versions of Pastoral*
   c. Spurgeon, *Shakespeare's Imagery*
   d. *The Oxford English Dictionary*
   e. Empson, *Seven Types of Ambiguity*

Follow one or several leading words through the play. (Examples: "measure," "eyes," "tongue," "stomach," "spirit," "sad," "mirth," "action," "wit" - there are many more which could profitably be studied.) What alternative meanings do they have? In what contexts is the potential fullness of meaning realized? When are they used (and by whom) in a restricted sense? How do they help to define character? to embody the major **themes** of the play?

8. Shakespeare's handling of plot.

See: a. Baldwin, *Five-Act Structure*
   b. Kitto, *Form and Meaning*
   c. Fergusson, *Idea of a Theatre*

How does the dramatist arrange the details of his story and with what results? (This might be better restricted to a single act or single scene.) How does Act I function as **exposition**? What else does it accomplish? How does Shakespeare suggest the passage of time? What is the dramatic function of such baffling scenes as Act I, Scene 2 or the first part of Act V, Scene 1?

9. The relationship of style and meaning. The use of verse and prose and the varying quality of the verse spoken by different characters or by the same character at different times. (This might include an analysis of the figures of speech used by one or more of the characters.)

See: a. Granville-Barker, *On Dramatic Method*
b. Sister Miriam Joseph, *Arts of Language*
c. Auerbach, *Mimesis*

What is the proportion of verse to prose in different parts of the play? What effect does this have on meaning? Analyze some of the longer verse speeches (particularly those of Friar Francis in Act IV). How does the quality of the speech help to define the character? (Quality refers here to such things as the use of **metaphor**, rhythm, density of language, and tone.) Does the "rhetoric" of some of Claudio's speeches (their 'high-flown" quality) say anything about his character? Is there a greater "density" (compactness, allusiveness, ambiguity) to the speeches of Benedick and Beatrice? What is the effect of this? What is the meaning of Dogberry's special "language"?

10. The problems of a production of *Much Ado About Nothing*. Read the play with an eye to the difficulties of staging particular scenes and of making dramatic sense (for a modern audience) of the "witty" dialogue. Consult the Variorum Edition for the statements of earlier actors and critics about the staging of the play. Look through recent volumes of the *Shakespeare Quarterly* for accounts of the latest productions of the play. Write an analysis of the problems confronting the producer.

11. The most important question - the meaning of the play. What is the plot center?

See: a. Fergusson, *Idea of a Theatre*
   b. Fergusson, *Human Image* ("Macbeth")
   c. Barber, *Festive Comedy*
   d. Kitto, *Form and Meaning*

The play is a complex arrangement of characters, actions, speeches, deceptions, and many other details. What underlying "action" (see "Appendix" in Fergusson's *Idea of a Theatre*) do all the characters mirror in their own ways?

www.ingramcontent.com/pod-product-compliance
Lightning Source LLC
LaVergne TN
LVHW011724060526
838200LV00051B/3016